D1071824

DREAM AND DEED

THE STORY OF

Katharine Lee Bates

DREAM AND DEED

THE STORY OF

Katharine Lee Bates

BY

DOROTHY BURGESS

UNIVERSITY OF OKLAHOMA PRESS

NORMAN

PUBLISHING DIVISION OF THE UNIVERSITY
COMPOSED AND PRINTED AT NORMAN, OKLAHOMA, U.S.A.
BY THE UNIVERSITY OF OKLAHOMA PRESS
FIRST EDITION

Dedicated to the memory of my father

ARTHUR LEE BATES

Acknowledgments

MANY FRIENDS of Katharine Lee Bates, acquaintances, correspondents, and persons now or formerly associated with Wellesley College have assisted me in the preparation of this memoir. To them my thanks and grateful appreciation are due. First, I am indebted to Miss Margaret Sherwood and Miss Martha Hale Shackford who generously gave their time to the reading of the manuscript. Their advice and encouragement and their intimate knowledge of Miss Bates's life and work provided much of the incentive and assistance without which I could not have completed the book.

I wish also to thank the following for many kindnesses, for patient reminiscence, suggestions, and verification of detail: Miss Vida Dutton Scudder; Miss Florence Converse; Mrs. Gamaliel Bradford; Miss Geraldine Gordon; Mrs. Harold E. Magnuson; Rev. Charles W. F. Smith; Miss Grace E. Arthur, secretary to the president of Wellesley College; Miss Helen Moore Laws; Miss Margaret M. Boyce; Mrs. Helen Swormstedt Mansfield, alumnae executive secretary, and her associates in the Wellesley College alumnae office; Mrs. Ruth Farrell of the Falmouth Free Library; members of my family; and others who kindly answered my many questions.

For permission to quote from letters and from published and unpublished material, I thank the following: The trustees of the Ella Lyman Cabot Trust, Incorporated; Mrs. Gamaliel Bradford; Mrs. Albert Payson Terhune; Leonard Bacon;

Miss Martha Hale Shackford; Miss Vida Dutton Scudder; Miss Florence Converse; Miss Geraldine Gordon; Miss Jeannette Marks; Mrs. Henry D. Holt; Miss Margaret Conklin, executrix of the estate of Sara Teasdale; John Foley, literary executor for Thomas S. Jones, Jr.; Mrs. Charles D. Woodberry; Norreys Jephson O'Conor; Wallace F. Hamilton; *The Wellesley Townsman*, *The Boston Herald*, and *The Springfield Republican*.

Many quotations from poetry and prose incorporated in the text are lines or sentences, often unidentified, written on blank pages of diaries, all of significance to Miss Bates.

DOROTHY BURGESS

Wellesley Hills, Massachusetts
March 25, 1952

The Chapters

The Illustrations

Dream and Deed

What of the deed without the dream? A song
Reft of its music, and a scentless rose.
Except the heart outsoar the hand, the throng
Will bless thee little for thy labor-throes.

The dream without the deed? Dawn's fairy gold,
Paled, ere it wake the hills, to misty gray,
Except the hand obey the heart, behold
Thy grievèd angel turns his face away.

Written in the choir of Wells Cathedral, 1890

DREAM AND DEED

THE STORY OF

Katharine Lee Bates

Katharine Lee Bates

painting by Mary Cotheal Burgess

I

The Family

In Falmouth, Massachusetts, about the year 1868, a young widowed mother gave a little red notebook to her small daughter Katie, a child of nine. Before putting it into the eager hands, she had made a few entries, ordinary jottings of her busy days that reveal much of her life and thoughts:

"Washed. Tried hard to get through early but did not accomplish it. . . . A quiet day with Jennie, puzzling her little head over the first conjugation of Latin verbs. . . . Attended church all day. Two excellent sermons. Very tired in the evening. . . . Went to a lecture by Rev. Mr. Clark of Yarmouth. Gave the origin of the Corinthian capital. . . . Set Dido on twelve duck eggs. Lady Blessington on thirteen. Jones and Princess on eleven each. . . . Received for quinces .25, for stitching .65. . . . Arthur's birthday, fifteen years old. I hope he is a true Christian. I called upon God."

After making these notes the hard-pressed mother, who was father as well to her four young children, perhaps found there was not time for the keeping of records, for she wrote to a sister-in-law, "Where is rest to be found in this weary world? I am growing a good deal in sympathy with the poor woman, who, when she was asked what was her idea of Heaven, said, 'to be able to put on a clean apron and sit down.' " Or perhaps Katie, picking up the little book with its gold lettering and blank pages, had begged her mother for it. Her name is written inside the cover, "Katie L. Bates," in faded childish script. She must have treasured this first little diary, for it has survived the years and the many family moves. No doubt, as time passed, she took it from a drawer in her study desk and smiled over the first entry:

"I am writing, scribbling rather, just for fun. Not that I have anything to say. There is a charm in bright, clean, unfilled pages, which I, for one, cannot resist. The lines are to short for good rhymes. Storys take up two many pages. So all I can do is to scribble. So I shall all over the book. Goodby dear imaginary audience."

Watching for the moments when the best opportunities for observation presented themselves, and taking pains to attract no attention, Katie silently judged the grown-up world and her position and that of her schoolmates in it. To her diary she confided her very definite conclusions and opinions:

"Women," she wrote, "are vixens or old maids or ladies. The worst is an old maid. The vixen next worse. A ladie perfect. . . . When men are married they are not so lonely as a general thing as a class of men called bachelors. Men who have lost their wives are called widowers. Men think they are more important than women. Some men call themselves gentlemen. There are some rough gentlemen though, I think. . . . Women are the feminine gender. They are highspirited as a general thing and I am happy to say have become impatient under the restraint men put upon them. So the great question of womens rights has arisen. I like women better than men. I like fat women better than lean ones. Some women call themselves ladies. . . . Girls are a very necessary portion of creation. They are full as necessary as boys. Girls (except a speches called tomboys) play with dolls when young. Afterwards croquet, games, etc. take up their spare time. Sewing is always expected of girls. Why not of boys. Boys don't do much but outdoor work. Girls work is most all indoors. It isn't fair. . . . Revenge is sweet. Mary L. Davis. M. Silvia Donaldson. I will tease, plague, provoke, outrage Mary in every possible way. She was in fault this time. I will take the other a bunch of flowers, for I am in fault."

So the "scribbling" began, and the little girl for her "private reading" wrote down her thoughts in the first of a long series of diaries. Katharine Lee Bates was to fill many notebooks with pages wide enough for "good rhymes" and for "storys" not too long for her patience. Writing was in her blood, for on both sides of her family writing and publishing were everyday occupations. Uncles and aunts poured out sermons, articles, lectures, and poetry, writing as naturally as they talked.

The parents of this small diarist were William and Cornelia Frances Lee Bates, who came to Falmouth in 1858. William had prepared for the Congregational ministry at Andover Theological Seminary after graduation from Middlebury College. Following two years of teaching, writing, and travel, he was installed in his first parish at Northbridge in 1845, and here he met and fell in love with the young Mount Holyoke graduate who had left her Northampton home to begin a teaching career in a small school in the village of Uxbridge, a few miles away. In response to Cornelia's request for advice upon the subject of her romance, her father wrote to her:

"I certainly should not object to your forming an alliance with a Gentleman with whom you could be not only *paired*, but *matched*. I should not object to the profession of which you spoke, for I believe it would be more congenial to your feelings, and that you are admirably calculated to fill such a station. At the same time I would wish you not to marry a Clergyman merely because he is a Clergyman, a poor miserable dolt of a thing, who might be considered pretty bright if he had sense enough to know that he was not fit for one. The person of whom you speak we, of course, know nothing of personally, therefore at present cannot give much advice about it, from what little we can pick up I should think it might be a very suitable match provided the disparity in your ages is no objection to you. I think it very commendable in him, as well as wise and judicious to give and take time to consider so serious and important a subject, that neither need be deceived in the other." And a few days later, when second thoughts had occurred to the anxious father: "Ascertain whether your Mr. B. is a *Loco Foco* or (what is worse) a *Liberty Party 'folks,'* as I should be mortified to be so nearly connected with one belonging to either of those parties. I cannot bring myself to think that an honest intelligent person can belong to the former and advocate and support an administration that can wage such a *ruthless, barbarous, murderous, unjust, uncalled-for* war as the Mexican War, in which we are now engaged, to say nothing of the acts which operate against the prosperity and well-being of our own country. As to the latter I think it the most corrupt party on earth, having the least of real abolition in it of any party in existence, a merely *political party* assuming the garb of religion to cover the basest purposes. You may think this strong language, but the time requires one to be explicit, and you very well know that I have the credit of always speaking so as not to be misunderstood."

Samuel Lee's correspondence was not with his daughter alone. Replying to a letter from his future son-in-law he wrote:

My dear Sir:

Yours of the 5th inst. received. I have delayed an answer thus long for want of time. The "advertisement" was Boxed May 12 according to your request, and according to Law in such cases made and provided. I can assure you that I consented to my daughter's leaving the paternal roof not without a pang; among the minor reasons her age and inexperience, not being sufficiently versed in domestic affairs—but in other respects, her talents, education, disposition, amiableness and desire to do all the good she can, admirably fits her for the station she is soon to occupy, viz. that of a minister's wife (which by the way I have more than once been told is no sinecure). . . . That her natural capacity is somewhat above mediocrity, I think cannot be denied, but, if she has attained a degree of maturity, uncommon at her age, I think the cause will be found, chiefly in her indomitable industry and perseverance. It has indeed been said that a child will be smart, if it has a smart mother, no matter what her father may be (which I do not exactly subscribe to) yet candor obliges me to say that whatever of extra natural talent she possesses, she must have inherited from her mother, though this is more than I have ever owned before. You were informed, I believe, of her origin and Family connexions in due season and, of course, cannot be disappointed on the score of Blood and Wealth, the latter of which is very convenient and desirable to anyone possessing it, but the former I think little of, it has never been my aim to crowd my family above what some call their own lives, but rather to fit them to be useful and respectable in the world, and thus fulfill their destiny, as they best may. And now, my dear sir, under all the circumstances, if you think the connexion a desirable one, take her—take her as the best earthly gift Heaven can bestow upon you, cherish her as your equal, she has a large and sound heart as poor humanity will admit, a soul not to be confined to this poor spot of earth, but that would be glad to grasp the universe, I mean as far as knowledge is concerned, but she has a frail body that will demand your kindest care and attention, your sympathies in sickness, share her joys, and divide her sorrows, and work with her on an even yoke and after having faithfully served your day and generation, and fulfilled the object of your creation and union, may you be received into that world where they neither marry nor are given in marriage.

Not at all discouraged by this letter from Cornelia's father, and having satisfied him upon the subject of politics, the young minister and Cornelia, who was undisturbed by the difference in their ages (ten years), were married at Northampton and began their lives together on the hill at Northbridge. Here were born their first four children, William, who died in his fifth year, Arthur Lee, Jane, and Samuel Lee. After twelve years, William terminated his pastorate at Northbridge and accepted a call to the church at Falmouth. He considered the move a fortunate one, for he was looking ahead to his children's schooling, and he and Cornelia heard with interest of Falmouth's Lawrence Academy which Falmouth boys and girls attended after graduation from the lower schools. To these young college graduates the education of their children was of first importance.

In William's family higher education began with his father, Joshua, a son of Zealous Bates who had been a farmer, a dealer in English and West Indian goods, a soldier of the Revolution, and, like his ancestors, a resident of Cohasset. In his father's store and on the farm Joshua was an able and much-needed assistant. Only a very little time was spared to him, therefore, for education—a few months a year as a day pupil in a private school for girls until he was eight years old, and after that even less time each year until he was seventeen. During this time he alternated between a desk in a small school conducted by his father and the counters of the store. When he was seventeen an accident to his right wrist incapacitated him for farm work. He then resolved that he would obtain a formal education and arranged to study alone under the supervision of the Reverend Josiah Shaw of Cohasset and the Reverend Henry Ware (who later became a professor at Cambridge).

Since Joshua's father could not meet the expense of a Harvard education, his son determined to earn as much as he could toward that end, and by "teaching in a private school, trapping muskrats, loaning the proceeds of sheep on shares and other similar ways" he was able to save $270 by 1797, when he entered Harvard as a sophomore. He was then twenty-one. For the next three years he supported himself by teaching and graduated with highest honors in 1800, the valedictorian of his class. In his class were such well-known graduates as Washington Allston, Joseph Stevens Buckminster, Charles Lowell, and Lemuel Shaw.

From Harvard, Joshua went to Phillips Academy at Andover, where he continued to teach while he studied theology. He was licensed to preach by the Andover Association and was ordained in 1803 at Dedham. He remained there for fifteen years, then resigned his pastorate to become president of Middlebury College. He was inaugurated just prior to his forty-second birthday, and in the same year he received the degree of Doctor of Divinity from Yale.

Of the seven sons of Joshua and his wife, Anna Poor of Andover, two died in infancy. The others were all educated at Middlebury and devoted their lives to law, education, journalism, or the ministry. The seven daughters were taught at home by their father and, with their brothers' assistance, undoubtedly received equivalent educations. Singly and in pairs the girls went to Charleston, South Carolina, where they taught in a private school for young ladies established by Mary, the eldest, under the patronage of their father's friend, John C. Calhoun. Events of the early months of the Civil War made it necessary to close the school, and since the marriages of four of the sisters depleted the teaching staff, it was reopened only briefly in later years. From all these sisters, from the brothers in Boston and in the South, and from the brothers by marriage who were doctors and professors, letters came to William, the clergyman brother in Massachusetts, and visits were made at intervals.

From the Lee side of the family, too, Cornelia's children inherited an intellectual bent. Her mother, Electa Bacon, was born in 1797 in Conway, Massachusetts, near the town of Buckland, where Mary Lyon was born in the same year. The two young girls must have known one another, and Electa doubtless followed Miss Lyon's career as an educator with interest. Electa's husband, Samuel Lee, a farmer and manufacturer of tin and pewter ware, found time to read his Shakespeare, and his worn and annotated one-volume edition of the plays still exists to bear witness to his close study. He and Electa must have been proud and happy to see their daughters graduating from the Female Seminary (later Mount Holyoke College) which Miss Lyon established at South Hadley.

Cornelia's pride (a trait her father had neglected to mention in his letter to his future son-in-law) was often sorely tried in her life as a minister's wife. William did not receive his salary regularly at Northbridge. In December, 1853, $58.00 was still due from April. Two hundred and fifty should have been paid in October, and by December another $125 was owed the uncomplaining young minister. In discouragement Cornelia wrote to her parents: "What can a poor man do? I mean to be thankful and believe that, if we can do our duty, we shall dwell in the land, and verily we shall be fed." Plans for a donation, distasteful enough to the young couple, were abandoned, and in March Cornelia wrote again: "The donation has flatted out to a 'Social Entertainment' to be given in the vestry by the ladies of the Congregational Society, admission 12 cts. Avails to be given to the Rev. William Bates. We are both feeling quite hurt that an able-bodied man, who earns his support, and who has never asked anything but his dues, should be thus held up as an object of charity, without his consent, for we knew nothing of it, till Mr. Bates saw the printed handbills stuck up in the Post Office, and I suppose they have been sent all over the region.

I don't want to show myself there, but Mr. Bates says I must go, for the people mean well. I have no reason to doubt this, but it is mortifying that they don't know any better what propriety consists in. However, I suppose the deacons will 'have a fiddle there' and it will go off somehow. I tell him I don't see what he can say, on the occasion, unless he prays for grace to bear all His ministrations with Christian meekness."

Poor proud Cornelia! For four more years she did her best, and it was with thankful hearts that the family packed their goods and left Northbridge for Falmouth and the prospect of regular income and security.

II

"The Loveliness of Love"

WILLIAM was not destined long to serve his new pulpit, for illness was already undermining the bright hopes for the future. Early in the year following the move to Falmouth he was attacked by severe pain in the back of the neck. At first the doctors diagnosed the condition as rheumatism, but in a very short time it became apparent that he was seriously ill. He had suffered a strain some sixteen years before and another ten years later while assisting fellow-passengers on a train which was disastrously wrecked in Rhode Island. It was believed that his illness resulted from these two occurrences. His suffering, which lasted many months, shadowed the life of the elder son, Arthur, who some seventy-nine years later wrote of his father's last months and death:

"I clearly remember the day my father died. The yard was crowded full of parishioners and other friends, all hoping that he might live. I was taken to the home of a neighbor who lived next door to the church, Mr. Gould, and couldn't understand why I was not permitted to go fishing down at Shiverick's Pond. I remember standing beside my father when the only way he could get any relief from intense pain was by standing upright. I remember *riding* to the cemetery and watching other boys *walk*. My mother once told me that Dr. Mackie, a young New Bedford physician, was the only one who suggested tumour, his opinion not being accepted by others. He and Dr. Rogers of Falmouth conducted the autopsy and Dr. Mackie was proved right. A 'small fibrous tumour at the third vertebra within the spinal column' was discovered and removed. They were so intent on their work that they did not notice the eight-year-old boy who stood at the foot of the bed and watched the whole operation."

This was Cornelia's year of mourning. In letters to her parents are glimpses of her husband's character, his strict observance of every duty and obligation, his eager way of recounting the details of his trips from home, his care for the children, his hours spent in teaching them to swim and fish, his attention to their lessons, and his unflagging patience and sweetness under all the vexations of his daily tasks.

But the year of mourning was also one of rejoicing, for Cornelia's fifth child was born a month before the father's death, and he had the joy of seeing the little Katie, who was to be her mother's greatest comfort in these first years of widowhood. Cornelia named the baby for her sister Catherine Lee, but chose a different spelling. This sister remained with Cornelia through all the months of William's illness and was her namesake's first nurse.

Once more in Falmouth, as in Northbridge, Cornelia pocketed her pride and in her extremity and for her children's sake accepted help, but now there were relatives in a position to assist her, for it was then customary for the family to help a clergyman member or his widow and children until the children were old enough to assume the burden.

Although grief had darkened the Falmouth home, the fatherless baby girl began her life under happy auspices. She was fortunate in her sturdy English ancestry, in her devoted immediate circle, and in her birthplace, the lovely little seaport of which she later wrote:

Here, too, where all were neighbors and hand lay warm in hand,
Where like our pink mayflower with brown leaves piled above,
Plain ways hid finest feeling, a child might understand
The loveliness of love.

The sea losses that robbed many a village home of a father or a son, the tragedy of the Civil War, the shock of the assassination of Abraham Lincoln—all made their impression upon Katie's mind, but no real sorrow, save Cornelia's widowhood, touched the four children. Gently refusing the offer of a sister-in-law to take Jennie temporarily, or even permanently, the courageous young mother kept her boys and girls together. With her older sister, Jennie, who was always "my little Sis," and the two brothers, Arthur, described by his mother as "stubborn and contumacious," and Sam, six years younger, Katie lived those early untroubled years, sheltered and secure in an environment where there was little money but much love. It was a wholesome environment, for strength of character was developed in all the children as they shared in the homemaking. A spirit of helpfulness, of sacrifice, of joy in contributing to the whole developed naturally. Though there was only corn-meal mush and molasses for the evening meal, it was thankfully received, and afterwards, with the circle of lamplight on the table, there were games or lessons with which the older children helped the younger, and there was always the mother around whom family life revolved and who encouraged, advised, and praised generously as she led her children into the paths of rectitude and responsibility.

As means and necessities dictated, the family moved five times during the years at Falmouth. Cornelia had a small yearly sum from the Massachusetts Congregational Society, and she was assisted by her brothers-in-law and by her own brother in Northampton. But she was not content to depend entirely upon relatives, however generous they were. She sewed for her neighbors, sold what produce she could raise, and found customers for her eggs and poultry. And the whole family "tied tags," as many people did in those days, for the Dennison Manufacturing Company, whose agents placed the work in the small towns.

Arthur considered himself the head of the family from the moment on the night of his father's death when he slowly and soberly wound the hall clock for the first time. With Sam he took what share he could of the responsibility, but the little brother was still a baby when William died, and for some years Arthur was alone in his efforts. He picked cranberries, drove cows, caught herring to sell to the fishermen for bait, and trapped muskrats for the skins, which brought thirty cents apiece. In addition to the small sums the boys were able to earn, they brought their mother wild duck and bluefish for her table and, in season, what berries could be spared from those picked to be sold. Proud as Cornelia was of her "brace of boys" she must have spent many an anxious hour when they were caught in a thunder shower out in the sound in a small fishing boat, or were late home from the woods with their guns and game.

Katie was concerned least of all the family with financial worries. With her seat-mate, Hattie Gifford, she studied her lessons at the village school and in the old burying ground, their favorite retreat, invented games or played house under the lilacs where the leaves of the silver poplar served as money. For more strenuous pastimes they hunted turtles in the swamp or organized battles, using pods of the catalpa tree for swords. Katie later wrote of herself in those days: "She was a shy near-sighted child, always hiding away with a book. It was in vain that unclothed dolls were given her to beguile her into sewing. She would promptly spin a romance that left them wrecked on a desert isle and obliged to wrap themselves in raiment of oak leaves secured by thorns and grasses." Memories of that happy time remained fresh in Katharine's mind, and many years afterward she wrote to Hattie: "Here we are at our old game of living still, though we have had our moments of wanting to go home. Perhaps we will go together, playing along the road as we used to do. Do you suppose there is a white-leaved bush on the way?"

But it was not all play for the little girl in a family where the children must very early learn severe lessons and understand and share grown-up sorrows and anxieties. An inwardly rebellious but obedient Katie went out to the fields and picked for her mother silver weed and pennyroyal to make a balm for a neighbor's rheumatism; a bewildered Katie learned her catechism at her mother's knee and tried the fires of hell as she held a candle flame to her small fingers; and a frightened five-year-old Katie hid under the lilacs and wondered why God had not turned aside a bullet in a darkened Washington theater. The memory of that day was always vivid. Late in her life she wrote of the sea captain who came home by stagecoach from Boston, bringing the newspaper which confirmed the rumor that had shocked the village. She described the memorial service in the church hung with widows' shawls as funeral draperies, for the one small store could not supply material. Her mother's shawl hung there among the rest.

Hattie and Katie remained close friends through all their lives, and Katie's gay little notes came to their old home, sent back from many journeys—often some bit of nonsense written when she was too tired or rushed for a real letter:

Dear Miss Hattie—

My true name is Fritillary though the children call me snakes-head. I'm usually purple like this, but occasionally white, and I grow in Iffley meadows, about two miles from Oxford. And May Day morning all good Oxonians get up at four o'clock and go to hear the Magdalen choristers sing a Latin hymn at five o'clock from the top of the Magdalen tower. Then the good people walk to Iffley and gather me and my kinsfolk and so "bring home the May." Thus did K.L.B. this morning and is so sleepy this afternoon that she can hardly hold the pen. So I'm writing for her and desire to express not only my love, but that of the skylark who nested close to my slender stem.

Affectionately
Fritillary

Falmouth and the old friends drew Katharine back all her life. She remembered always the note of the "holy bell of Paul Revere" in the steeple of her father's church mingling with the crying of the gulls over the

fair sea-village, wrapt in its pearly haze,

where there first came to her

through all human cherishment
Hints of the far divine.

Here in Falmouth Katharine received the "gift of mirth." Here too she first saw sorrow as she watched neighbors wait in vain for sailors who would not return. Here she tasted first the "sacrament of life," a life that in its outer aspects was contained by the village and by the sea which she was to watch on many coasts. Stretching away in restless mystery beyond the Elizabeth Islands, beyond the Vineyard, and still beyond distant Nantucket, she knew it then only in its familiar nearness on the Falmouth beaches. Remembering that "ever-surging sea" she later apostrophized it:

But O my ocean, O my saddest, bravest,
Forever flinging thy wild heart away,

Forever forced from the land thou cravest
By secret laws thy being must obey!
Thine is it still to strive and fail and long;
But where hath earth a music like thy song?

Katie's love of the sea took deep root early in her life, and references to it are to be found in many of her poems. How glad she was to learn in time that she was of a line of Kentish folk beyond the "sea-path"—folk who took with them the "brief blunt name" from one seabound land to another. During a pilgrimage to Lydd, "far away on the sunny levels," she wrote home, for publication by the Bates Family Association, a fanciful account of a visit made to Clement, the emigrant ancestor, by all of his invisible future descendants:

"Ancestor Clement heaves a sigh; then he suddenly turns and stares at us. Surprised at our numbers, for we overflow house and garden and orchard, as a flock of rooks might settle on Romney Marsh, he is encouraged by our shadowy presence. 'As you will, wife,' he says to Ann in patient voice. 'Not yet, not this year nor next nor for half a dozen more, mayhap, but go we must and shall. There are those over in America that look for us.' "

Of all those undreamed-of descendants, none was to be more mindful than the adult Katharine of the debt to the "glimmering crew of dear and queer ancestral ghosts" who shaped the deeds and moods of the future bearers of the name, who colored their hair and fashioned their noses, who gave her her sea-love and her dreams, and who spoke again in her conscience.

Falmouth, when Katharine lived there, was about sixteen miles from the nearest railroad. But there was no sense of isolation, for it was a busy little port, linked with the great world by the seafaring men, and sometimes their wives, who came and went on their far voyages, bringing the unknown

Mrs. William Bates

Reverend William Bates

Katharine Lee Bates

Jane Bates

Arthur Lee Bates

Samuel Lee Bates

shores and cities into their homes with their tales and their sea chests, in which were packed, as Katie recalled in later years, shells, coconuts, tamarinds, dates,

luscious sweetmeats pressed
Into blue jars of quaint pagoda dome,

corals, shimmering shawls, and ivory carvings. Sometimes they brought back living testimony of their South Sea Island cruises, when Kanaka boys came home with them to remain until another voyage, receiving what education they could absorb and teaching the Falmouth boys to swim with their own ease and skill and to shoot with bow and arrow.

Katie observed the life of the town from her particular vantage point. She led the rather confined life of little girls of her day, did the indoor work she did not care for, and listened to the exciting talk of her brothers, who went off on the "Emily Mac" to New Bedford, or on rare occasions by steamer to Marthas Vineyard and Nantucket. The elder brother, who was bearing responsibility so young, still had time to watch over and care for his little sister. Among his many memories he recalled very clearly the day a peddler passing by the house stopped briefly and removed from his pack a pair of spectacles which he perched on the bridge of Katie's small nose. Looking up wonderingly, she cried, "Why, there are leaves on those trees!"

Death was often spoken of in Cornelia's circle of family and friends. There were the many losses at sea of Falmouth men, and Cornelia's widowhood was always apparent, for she never wore colors after her husband's death. Too, there was the burying ground, Katie's rendezvous with Hattie, where together they traced the weathered epitaphs, "muffled in moss and lichen-overgrown" and spelled out the names of those lying under the grasses and the untended vines. These experiences must have impressed Katie quite early with an awareness of death, for while she was still at the village school she solemnly and carefully wrote out her first will, which was witnessed by her chief beneficiary and executrix:

My last will and testament

Will of KATIE L. BATES

I, Katie L. Bates, do hereby make my will, for life is uncertain. I give and bequeath all my worldly possessions in the way of dolls and toys to Hattie L. Gifford, with the wish that she will give them to poor indians. I also give and bequeath all my garments to my mother, Mrs. C. F. Bates, with the exception of my blue coat which I bequeath to my dear freind and classmate, Hattie L. Gifford. My schoolbooks I give and bequeth also to Hattie L. Gifford hoping she will profit by my numerous notes. To my dear, though provoking sister, Jane Bates, I give and bequeth my writing desk and all contained therein. To my older brother, Arthur L. Bates, I leave the old cat, with my love. To my younger brother, I bequeth my sizzors, thimble etc. with the hope he will learn to mend his britches. To my schoolmates I give and bequeth my love, and urge them to remember the words, "Life is uncertain." To Minnie Marion I give and bequeth a peice of paper which she will find between pages 324 and 325 in my History. To May Ida Shiverick I bequeth my spectacles and my blessing. My money that I have accumulated during my lifetime, I give and bequeth to Mrs. Sarah Lawrence, for cutting my hair. To my graceful freind, Dr. Everet, I give and bequeth my jackknife for tending me when I was sick. My story books and magazines I give to Hattie L. Gifford, as my executor, and if I have forgotten anything, I bequeth it to her. I give you all my blessing. Think not ill of the dead.

Witness Hattie L. Gifford N. Robinson

Katie's "scribbling" was not confined to her diary and her will. There were poems and stories, carefully signed "Katie L. Bates," and a few of these were saved by her mother. Perhaps the brothers and the "provoking sister" were not allowed to see these early compositions, but no doubt Hattie, in the retreat under the lilacs, thrilled to the

Romance of Count Hymbo

Count Hymbo was a gallint knight
Of honor and renown.
None braver was there in the fight,
Pride of his native town.

His limbs were long, and lank, and lean;
His body rather fat:
A nobler sight never was seen,
When on his steed he sat.

Count Hymbo felt so very big,
That he did quite disdain,
To fall in love—the stingy pig—
No one must share his fame.

But one night, as he slowly rode,
Through the forest dark and drear,
He passed a humble log abode.
"I'll get my supper here."

Now Hymbo was a cruel knight
Although he was so smart,
He used to kill men out of spite,
Stick his dagger through their heart.

Count Hymbo pounded at the door
Of the cottage in the wood,
A voice exclaimed, "O knock no more
Unless you mean us good."

Dream and Deed

"No matter what I mean to thee,
I am Count Hymbo brave.
So, open, stranger, unto me,
Or I'll send thee to thy grave."

At this the door did open wide,
Count Hymbo tied his horse,—
Then, entering the hut, he cried,
"I say, where is the boss?"

He lit a torch and gazed around,
And saw a maiden fair,
But she was gazing on the ground
With a look of deep despair—

The Count sat down and crossed his leg,
Then said with cruel leer,
"What is the matter, Miss, I beg?"
The maiden dropped a tear.

"Ah, sir, if you're a honest knight,
Pray go away from here,
Your presence fills me with affright."
She dropped another tear.

Hymbo gazed on her lovely face,
And on her golden hair.
He gazed in silence for a space,
And then he moved his chair.

"I'll put a question to you, Miss.
Say will you be my wife,
Look up, my dear, and answer this.
Or else I'll take your life."

"No," the maiden firmly said.
Count Hymbo's sword so true
Did in a minute lay her dead.
Count Hymbo grunted, "Whew!"

"The Loveliness of Love"

But the next night, at twelve o'clock
As Hymbo lay awake,
He saw what gave him such a shock
That every nerve did quake.

He saw a figure, robed in white,
Slowly approach his bed,
Trembled all over did the knight,
"You murderer," it said.

From his couch up started that knight,
His handsome face was deathly white,
The figure vanished from his sight,
And Count Hymbo died of fright.

Katie L. Bates

The twelve happy years slipped by, the only carefree years of Katharine's life. Cornelia saw her four children growing up in the fine atmosphere of the neighborly little town, and the three older children were proving themselves good scholars at Lawrence Academy. She soon relinquished any hope of further education for the boys. Arthur and Sam had their way to make and must put aside their books. But the tradition of learning was strong, and Cornelia, aided by her sister Catherine and by the letters from her husband's sisters, instilled an undying love for it in her sons and daughters.

III

Falmouth

EIGHT YEARS after William's death the first break came in the family group when Arthur left school and went to work in Northampton. His uncle, Samuel Lee, secured a place for him in a bookstore and invited him to live in his home. Arthur worked in the store for two years and boarded alternately with his employer and his uncle. Since he was paid only $50.00 a year, he could send back to Cornelia only very little money, but occasionally he sent oranges or candy, and he managed somehow to buy paper-backed copies of Charles Dickens' novels for Katie. Cornelia wrote to a sister-in-law during his absence: "I have never felt so lonely since William was taken away, as now. Arthur has become companionable and sympathetic to quite a degree for so young a child and I leaned upon him more than I was aware. Dear little fellow, I pity him. He is kept very busy, and says he often feels at night as if he could not drag himself home." Cornelia's pity would have turned to righteous indignation if Arthur had told her that he opened the store at seven in the morning, closed it at ten-thirty in the evening, did his employer's odd jobs, and carried fifty-pound bundles of binder board up three flights of stairs to the bindery above the store. He was a slight boy at that time, weighing less than 120 pounds, and it was no wonder that his feet could scarcely carry him home at night.

Arthur has described the incident which terminated this first venture into the world: "I worked hard during my two unhappy years in Northampton and became more and more resolved to give it up and go home. The end came when one hot day Mr. Bridgman bought a twelve quart pail of blueberries of a friend who had to drive past Mr. Bridgman's house on his way home and offered to leave them there. It was three quarters of a mile from the store. Probably I needed the discipline for Mr. Bridgman told me to carry the berries to his home and bring back the pail. I did and when I reached the store I threw it in the door and it went clattering across the floor to Mr. Bridgman's desk. I told him I wouldn't stand it any longer and was going to quit. I know I shouldn't have done it but I couldn't help it. Mr. Bridgman owed me twelve dollars and he finally paid it to me all in old-fashioned cents which he had been saving. That's the kind of a man he was. He wrote my mother a letter that made her very unhappy."

So Arthur came home to Falmouth disillusioned and discouraged and badly in need of a vacation. Sam, meantime, was taking Arthur's place as best he could. Jennie, who possessed some of the domestic traits that Katie lacked, was a help to her mother in the house. No doubt Katie had her share of the tasks, too, but she was still the baby of the family and escaped when she could to play with Hattie or, if the weather were unfavorable, invented interesting ways of making the time pass indoors, as on one occasion when she persuaded a reluctant Jennie to watch her drop the cat from an upstairs window to see if he would land on his feet. No matter how she was occupied, she was always listening to the talk around her watching the neighbors and guests who came and went, and absorbing more than her mother guessed of the letters that arrived regularly from the aunts and uncles.

Poetry must very early have become a part of her consciousness. Aunt Catherine's pleasant little verses, which found ready acceptance in the journals of the day, were enjoyed by the family, and of course the New England poetry of that golden age would have been loved and learned by Cornelia's children. But there was other literary fare always at hand, and Cornelia may have tried to read aloud and interpret the imposing red and gold volume of Joshua Bates's sermons, *Bates on Christian Character,* which had a conspicuous place on the parlor table. It may be that the first sermon, "Man Immortal and Accountable," planted in Katie's mind the unanswered question with which she was to be preoccupied all her life. To William, the only son to follow his father into the ministry, the volume had been especially precious, and Cornelia treasured it carefully.

The letters coming to Falmouth from a world that must have seemed very far away to Katie were full of interest, but even more interesting were the occasional visitors. The Congregationalist ministers who came to supply the pulpit or who were under consideration for the position of pastor were given room and board in Cornelia's home. They were subjected to a very intent consideration by the little brown-eyed girl who, with a keen feeling for detail, stored up her impressions until she was alone, when out came the red diary to capture the guest in its pages:

Ministers Entertained at the house of Mrs. Bates.

Rev. Mr. Moss, a missionary in foreign lands. Has a big, big stummark. Talks heathen fluently. Has wonderful children. Thinks old maids are a nuisance.

Rev. Mr. Beard. A very small man. Red Hair. White hands. In very poor health. Makes fun of my glasses. He and Mother are very sharp with each other. Has a baby he thinks is wonderful. Is afraid though proud of his wife.

Rev. Mr. Fellows. A big fat burly gruff kind of man. Laughs very loud. Talks incessantly. Has seven children. Feels big of his sermons. Very powerful sermons. Talks and looks like a regular rowdy. Feels big. Has blue eyes.

Rev. Mr. Harlow. A round man, full of fire and energy. Spirited. Is good speaker. A handsome person, an apt mimic. Interesting, merry, conversational. Tells many stories. Reads very much. Has been in bad health. Is better now. Blacks his boots hard. Laughs often.

Rev. Mr. Rich. A very polite good man. Still not calculated to enchant at the first sight. When he retires kisses me. Shakes hands with the others. Ditto when he leaves. Gave us a Bible lesson. Evidently has studied the Scriptures diligently. Knows a great deal I think.

Rev. Mr. Craig. Very fine man, not settled in the ministry. A wife. Preached as a candidate, was rejected. Felt very badly. Man of very fine sensibility, truthful, plain, conscientious, generous and rather handsome. Very heavy eyebrows. Carries himself very erect. To a stranger looks stiff. Noble gentleman.

Rev. Elijar Kellog. Very eccentric. Not settled in the ministry. Writes stories for boys. Very fond of boys. Very quick in all his motions. Impolite and rude. Says very queer things. Dresses carelessly. Has dirty fingers, dirty hands, dirty nails. Brown hands. Married.

Life in Falmouth seemed destined to continue uneventfully. Katie looked forward to further schooling, and Jennie talked of preparing herself to be a teacher. Arthur left home again, this time to go to Boston where he would stay with friends and look about for another position. Reluctant though she was to see him go, Cornelia felt a certain sense of relief, for Arthur, like many other Falmouth boys, had talked of going to sea. Boston was a far less terrifying prospect, and there he had uncles to extend a helping hand. A Mr. Cumings, the father of a boy William had tutored and fitted for college, was interested in Arthur and mentioned him to a neighbor who was president of a life-insurance company. This gentleman had suggested that the young man be brought to his house very early one morning when he would "have a look at him." As Arthur told the story: "Mr. Crocker's door was not locked and we went in. Mr. Cumings called, 'Where are you, Henry?' and I heard a voice say, 'Down cellar, Brad. Have you got that boy with you? Come down here.' Mr. Crocker was about six foot, three and very thin. His hair was white. He was without a collar or vest, had on a white shirt, black trousers and carpet slippers and had an axe in his hand. He towered over me and, not waiting for any introduction, said, 'Boy, can you split wood?' I had wit enough to say, 'Yes sir, I have split a good deal of wood for my mother.' 'That's good,' he said, 'I wouldn't give a damn for a boy that couldn't.' "

As a result of this informal interview with the alarming Mr. Crocker, Arthur went to work for the company with which he remained all his life, moving on from position to position until he became president. He later wrote of the occasion, "It seemed like Heaven compared with Northampton and I could hardly wait till night that first day so I could write my mother and tell her all about it."

How that letter was received may be imagined. Cornelia's relief and thankfulness were very great. Her hopes and prayers had followed her eldest. He was among friends and relatives, and he was earning not $50.00 a year, but $50.00 a month.

For two more years Cornelia's quiet life in the village continued, and then most unexpectedly the family was reunited, though not in Falmouth. Cornelia's sister Catherine had been making a long stay with friends in Grantville, Massachusetts (now Wellesley Hills). She had been in frail health for some years, and Boston physicians now advised her that she must henceforth live the life of an invalid. The Grantville friends owned a small white cottage next to their own home which they offered to Cornelia, rent free, so that she might establish a home with her sister where Catherine could remain close to her doctors. Cornelia accepted at once, and the momentous step was taken. Thus life in Falmouth ended and life in Wellesley began, with Arthur once more living at home. Sam very soon went to work in an organ factory, where he learned the business thoroughly and prepared himself for the time when he would establish his own factory. The girls started at their new school, and Cornelia assumed the added role of nurse for her invalid sister.

IV

The Dream of Wellesley

Aunt Catherine's last three years were happy ones. She was surrounded by love, and to the end her eager mind rejoiced in the bright promise of the lives of her nieces and nephews. Jennie (who had changed her name to "Jeannie," though she remained "Jen" to the family) was studying at the Framingham Normal School; Arthur and Sam, now dignified businessmen, were taking the seven o'clock train for Boston; and Katie was at Wellesley High School, then called Needham High School.

The frame high-school building is now a college dormitory and stands just within one of the entrances to the Wellesley campus. But when Katie and her friend Emily Norcross, who was to enter Wellesley with her, constituted the entire high-school class of 1874, it was situated on the main street of the village and was occupied by all the grades. The two girls walked to and from school together, accompanied by Emmie's two older brothers, who formed the class of 1873. Katie and Emmie marched the distance, shoulder to shoulder, faster and faster, until Emmie's thick yellow braid swung in the wind as they chanted "Lars Porsena of Clusium" and other stirring lines. There was always a pause for a rest at the little pond which, in a somewhat incomplete enthusiasm for French, they christened "Cheval Pond."

The Bates family moved to Grantville in the year of the founding of Wellesley College. The two sisters, Cornelia and

Catherine, college-bred and hopeful that a way would be found to give Katie the advantages of higher education, followed with deep interest the plans of Wellesley's founders, Mr. and Mrs. Henry Fowle Durant. Since Catherine lived only two miles from the college, she had heard from friends and neighbors the details of the plans going forward, and she had much to tell her sister when the work of settling in their new home was finished. To Cornelia, who had known the grief of losing a little boy, the story of Mr. and Mrs. Durant's tragedy in the death of their only child was especially poignant. Their ambition to found a college for women on the beautiful property they had originally acquired as an estate for their son filled her with admiration, and the project became in her home, as in others in the village, a main topic of conversation.

Katie's writing continued under the stimulus of her new surroundings and the encouragement of her aunt, who read and approved or criticized the careful little poems so like those she herself wrote. These verses or scraps of prose Cornelia no longer labeled "Katie's nonsense" as she gathered them lovingly and put them safely away, for Aunt Kate praised them and commended the studious tastes of her niece. The family began to realize that Katie was developing a true scholarly and literary bent, though she was still a village schoolgirl scrambling with her friends over the scaffolding of the great building rising on the hill which overlooked Lake Waban—the first of the buildings that were to become the "college in the woods." The faint dream of going to Wellesley became more and more vivid in Katie's mind. A character in one of her early stories soliloquizes as Katie must have, while walking home under the tall elms that met over Washington Street: "I would study and study. I would know what makes the beautiful colors around you, dear old setting sun, and I would learn all about the nations on the other side of the globe you are going to shine on now. I would know how the earth came to be, and all about the stars, and I would read the thoughts men wrote hundreds of years ago in strange letters and queer-sounding languages. I would find out why some poetry is poetry and some poetry isn't, and where the Garden of Eden was, and how my head thinks. I would study and study and study and know and know and know."

Catherine Lee died in September, 1874, a few months after Katie's graduation from high school. Her friends had other uses for the house, Katie was still unprepared for college, and the way was not clear financially. There was much to decide and plan. A move to Newtonville seemed a wise step for many reasons. The boys would be nearer Boston, and Jeannie would be nearer her Brighton school where she had begun to teach. Katie could enter Newton High School for two years of advanced work in preparation for college.

Life was easier in Newtonville, and little by little the family fortunes began to improve. Cornelia, always eager to share with others, could now give her mince pies to a passing peddler, or Jeannie's old cloak to the woman who sold baskets. Arthur, Sam, and Jen shared the family expenses, and since Arthur's yearly salary was now increased to $1,200, he felt that with patient self-denial he could spare the necessary $250 a year to assure Katie her college education. He was very proud of "Sife" (his nickname for Katie), and especially proud of her acceptance of his help only as a loan. Katie had been reared in the tradition which teaches that an obligation assumed is an obligation met; moreover, she was already seeing her poems and stories in print in her school papers and in the *Newton Journal*. This small success encouraged her to believe that she could repay her brother and perhaps share the expenses of the home at some future date.

Falmouth provided much of the material for Katie's early literary efforts. Although she had been only twelve years old when she left, her mind was filled with vivid memories of the village, of the changing seasons, of the woods and fields, of the marshes and the sea. The life of the village gave her stories, and her quick imagination wove drama from remembered incidents. Her descriptions were of Falmouth homes and customs, and her conversations were in the colloquial language. Her tales are storehouses of the authentic speech of a Cape Cod village of that time.

Katie was graduated from Newton in 1876. Wellesley College had been in existence for a year, and Katie's reputation as a student had preceded her there. Her graduation photograph shows her as befits a class poet of scholarly purpose: a serious young woman, plainly dressed, wearing conspicuous eyeglasses, her downward glance veiling the fun in her brown eyes. The frivolous flowers in her hair and at her throat were tucked there hastily by a classmate who took them from her own dress.

Before Katie entered Wellesley in the autumn, Cornelia had an opportunity to examine for herself this new college which was to provide for her daughter "the elevating and refining influences of a happy Christian home." Cornelia had no qualms on this score, for Katie had always lived in such a home. But she reflected somewhat anxiously upon the "appointments" of College Hall, which were to be "such as are usually found only in the abodes of the wealthy." Katie knew nothing of such abodes, though Cornelia had been able to create attractive surroundings for her children. Many of her father-in-law's fine pieces of mahogany furniture had come to her, and the bureaus with their swinging mirrors and brass knobs, the four-post beds, the drop-leaf tables, the graceful side chairs, and the deep, upholstered rockers had provided comfort, if not elegance. There were bright carpets, patchwork quilts, books, and lamplight catching the gleam of the Sandwich glass marbles on William's old round marble board to give warmth and color. The engravings of religious subjects in plain frames ornamented the walls and reminded one that this was a minister's home. If only William might have lived, Cornelia thought, to see his youngest a Wellesley freshman —one of the fortunate few to be accepted for the great new college.

As Cornelia compared the simplicities of her home with the handsomely furnished rooms in the great building which the College Calendar described as "the most beautiful and perfect in the world for the education of woman," she rested her faith upon the level head and discriminating taste of her daughter, and also upon the single-minded purpose which would tend to make Katie indifferent to her physical environment. There probably were some details of that environment which obtruded themselves upon Katie's consciousness; she was to wear flannel underwear in all seasons, since only flannel or silk were permitted, and Cornelia could not afford silk. Cotton was not recommended or allowed. And there would be no confectionary or irregular eating. There could be only the three meals a day of "varied and nutritious food." Poor Katie had so loved evenings in a friend's home when a molasses candy pull was in order. Now all her evenings were to be spent in College Hall. Except for vacation periods, only once in the four years did she step outside the hall after seven o'clock in the evening. On this occasion the girls were directed to form in line and march two by two as, watched over by members of the faculty, they moved in orderly fashion to the conservatory. There they were led past the night-blooming cereus, and then back up the hill to their rooms, awed or rebellious as the case might be. Many years later the eyes of another member of the class of 1880 would flash with annoyance at the recollection. In 1876 these rules, all designed for her daughter's good, troubled Cornelia not at all.

The carefree summer slipped swiftly by, and the autumn

Birthplace of Katharine Lee Bates
Falmouth, Massachusetts
(larger house on the right)

Katharine Lee Bates
in 1876

day came when Katie forsook the rooftree, settled her few possessions in the plain bureau and modest wardrobe allotted to her, and began the life at Wellesley which was to flow on with scarcely a break for as long as she lived.

College Hall was indeed a luxurious home, with steam heat, gas lighting, elevator, carpets, rugs, carved chairs with embossed leather seats and backs, cushioned wicker settees, paintings in wide frames, busts and statues, and the great palm-filled Center from which tiered balconies rose to the roof.

Cornelia gave thanks for all the glorious opportunities devised by Mr. Durant and opened to her daughter—the varied courses, the boating, the calisthenics, the daily hour of light domestic work (a discipline highly approved, but not by Katie). In this atmosphere, designed to "make the life of the student refined and noble," Katie would receive an education equal to those for men.

In Cornelia's long and lonely service to her children many a milestone had been passed. Now the future of the youngest was assured. Slowly the threads were weaving the pattern of Katie's life—the griefs, the impulsive acts, the faithful tasks performed, the "unconsidered trifles" that take on significance in later years. William's premature death, the empty blueberry pail thrown angrily on the floor, the need of one sister for another, a boy's effort to keep a kitchen woodbox filled—all had drawn together in the warp and weft of a life that was to belong to the unguessed dream of a great college.

V

The Class of '80

DURING Katharine's undergraduate years College Hall was the only building on the campus, except for the East Lodge and Mr. and Mrs. Durant's home, both on Washington Street. Remote in its great wooded acreage, it stood high on the hill, surrounded on three sides by the beautiful estate whose natural loveliness had been enhanced by landscaping. On the fourth side was Waban Mere, a sheltered lake which Katharine later wished "would give back to human visions only once the faces that have been mirrored in his waters—the tawny Indian faces that looked gravely down from birch canoes, and the host of Wellesley faces, girlish, hopeful, dreamy faces, that have leaned from boat or bank above him." Here was "a Paradise still fresh and wild . . . meadows and hillsides rich with blossoms, those violets, anemones, columbines, lady-slippers, whose profusion hardly survived one generation." Only a grassy path or two led away from the main driveways, to Tupelo, the wooded point in the lake which early became a favorite campus retreat; to the hill where Stone Hall and Olive Davis Hall now stand, but where Katie in her day buried herself in pine needles to her chin for protection from the cool air and read Livy; or to the other hill, crowned now by Green Hall, where she found a "perfect wilderness amid the tangled boughs and bushes."

But for all Wellesley's fair aspect of wood and water, the real college to which Katie came and to which she gave her life's allegiance was the unseen college of aspiration. For Katie the heart of the college was the library, a "long, dim room" with "the browns and crimsons of the volumed shelves . . . the long, green tables and the careless chairs." Her hours in the library set the course of her life; the habits of the scholar grew upon her there, as well as the concept of fellowship which, in spite of her intermittent longing for solitude, became one of the fixed stars by which she lived. In Wellesley's library she sensed the great fellowship of those who labor in the vineyards of the mind and whose fruits lay all about her within the grasp of her hand. To her they became "the laurelled brotherhood . . . the kings of thought and the emperors of dream." Here she became aware that

Visions shall come and go
On the dreaming eyes of Youth,
And here shall her chosen know
The countenance of Truth.

Next in interest was the Browning Room, where Katie would retreat to a quiet corner and allow the poetic influences of the room to play upon her receptive consciousness. There were poems in manuscript, original letters, cabinets of choice bric-a-brac, a marble bust of Mrs. Browning, and other pieces of sculpture. Scattered all about were comfortable chairs and convenient tables, and the heavy portieres at the windows created a hush that made the room seem withdrawn from the rest of the building.

When the first confusion was over, the courses planned, and the domestic duties allotted, the forty-three members of the class of 1880 swiftly drew together in the new bonds of friendship and loyalty to their group. They appointed a committee of five, of which Katie was one, to frame their constitution. When their officers were chosen they elected her their perpetual president, an honor and distinction which meant more to her than any other in her long life. With maidenly modesty they chose white for their badge, but before long one of the more adventurous classmates persuaded them to change to scarlet, and the flaming color proclaimed the glory of '80 at every future reunion. They adopted for their motto *Pondere Non Numero*. Then, with their parliamentary forms properly completed, they settled down to a new and crowded life. So began the fellowship of '80 honored in Wellesley annals.

The class was closely knit, but of all the girls Marion Pelton became especially dear to Katie. Circumstances kept the two near one another all their lives, and a deep sympathy and understanding bound them in a friendship which joined them in their classmates' thoughts always. Their private signature was two linked circles, Polonius' "hoops of steel." Marion, herself a sensitive poet, became Katie's best critic.

The class of 1879 held the distinction of being Wellesley's first class, but the second was not content merely to walk upon ground already broken. They would tread new paths wherever possible. In their initial class meetings they organized the first glee club and the first boating crews. The glee club achieved such excellence that it performed at many a college function. The crews, in numbers that filled the available seven boats and left a disconsolate group to sit on Waban's banks and applaud their classmates' seamanship, were earnest but ineffective Undines, Evangelines, Mayflowers, and Jumblies under "monstrous hats," as they rowed in all directions, sometimes stern foremost. Katie composed a boating song which won the offered prize.

Not content with the societies organized for them by Mr. Durant—the Shakespeare Society and the Greek letter societies—they formed, with members of the class of 1879, Wellesley's first literary society and enlisted the interest of the founder. But their hope that it would perpetuate itself was not realized.

In their senior year they proposed a Wellesley cheer, but to Ada Howard, the first president of the college and an honorary member of the class, a boisterous cheer echoing across the meadows on the occasion of class-day exercises was not to be thought of. Miss Howard's opinion perforce went undisputed and later in the day she congratulated them upon the "refined, high-toned and learned" nature of the class-day program.

When Katie's freshman year ended she went gladly home to Newtonville to her mother's cooking and a hammock swung under the trees, but she welcomed with no enthusiasm her mother's gift of a biography of the mathematician, Nathanial Bowditch. Tired and unwilling to return to the labors of education, she wrote rebelliously to a classmate: "How this vacation wears away! I don't want to go back to Wellesley; all my former aversion to the 'nashty old place' has returned in full force. I feel abusive toward the class of '80, and I would sooner iron the Phi Sigma flat than crown her queen with laurel green. As for Mr. Durant, I wish him peace a hundred miles away. The third part of Algebra gibbers on my nightmares, and as for my Greek, I have forgotten the alphabet. I don't want to work. I would like to swing in the hammock with a book forever. But what treason for eighteen!"

In a retrospective mood she reviewed her eighteen years for her classmate—the first six misty miles of flowers and thorns, milk and honey, when a fat little girl in a blue sunbonnet draped a legless doll on a sapling; six clearer miles of rougher road where Dickens characters and colonies of shells and marbles lined the way, and where she begged Hattie Gifford to lock her in an empty tomb and then become the angel of resurrection to lead her off to judgment; then six still clearer miles of stony uphill climbing, littered with brown-papered books, ink-spattered and spotted with kerosene, and with fragments of eyeglasses gleaming on the path. At the last she saw herself, sitting with her knees drawn up under her dress, staring at the fog, knowing that at nineteen a fairer but shadowed country awaited her. Later that summer she wrote with some asperity of a teacher who actually had a framed photograph of Edward Olney, the author of *Olney's University Algebra*, hanging on her wall. This teacher, Katie claimed, "would, if Caligula were alive, put his toga into a patchwork quilt."

In spite of this first-vacation mood Katharine was at heart a dedicated young woman, taking for her ideal that devotion to truth which Mr. Durant had from the first determined should be the lofty aspiration of his college. Katharine soon became his loyal admirer. In time she heard echoes of criticism still circulating from the years before his son's death and his old-fashioned conversion, but she paid no heed to gossip and accorded him her fullest admiration, believing intensely in his "spirit of self-forgetful love, of faith in God, of discipleship to Christ." Since she was innately modest herself, Mr. Durant's self-effacement in refusing to lend his name to the college or to present it with bust or portrait effectively nullified in her mind his autocratic ways. His unwearying efforts to bring beauty in every manifestation into the college won her lifelong devotion to the man. She later described his intellectual leadership as "generous in sympathy, daring in aspiration, sound in scholarly principle, restless and aggressive." His attention to Wellesley ranged from the beautifying of the landscape to the carving of a balustrade or the shaping of a bureau handle. She knew him well, for there were so few students at Wellesley in the early years that everyone became well acquainted with the founder, who was to be encountered on the path or around the turn of a corridor at any time. Katharine took Mr. Durant's words as her creed in her devotion to Wellesley: "Gather around it all wisdom and all knowledge. Bring to it the light of all science and all truth. Study over it; pray over it; live in it; love in it; suffer for it." She did not fail to fulfill each one of these admonitions.

The undergraduate years hurried on to become in memory a colorful kaleidoscope of class meetings, parties, picnics, Chinese lanterns, Japanese parasols, lemonade, ice cream, prize poems, midnight confidences—all set against a background of hard study, which was, of course, the major occupation of Katharine's student days. Although her chosen subjects were English and Greek, she bore the discipline of the required mathematics and sciences and found that her schedule allowed ample time for the history and languages which rounded out her formal education. She managed to find opportunity for poems and stories, as well. She wisely wrote only of what she knew, and she used the poetic diction of the day, experimenting in many stanza forms. The New England poets were her models, but much of her verse is reminiscent of the long musical lines of Swinburne, which especially appealed to her. She found it easy to slip into the style of a dozen poets, with the result that her poems were smooth and facile but without marked distinction, although an occasional line showed a growing power of imagination:

The lifted skies
Are royal with old goddesses and queens,
Whose faces lit the earth,

. . . .

The hoarse, wet wind on his ragged way
Mocks the leaves in their tarnished gold.

At Wellesley Katharine's awareness of nature was enhanced, and her poems, only a very few of which she later preserved in collected editions of her verse, are full of gracefully conceived images, faultless in their accuracy. Nothing escaped her loving observation, and she delighted in the growing sureness of her touch.

Wellesley had no undergraduate paper or magazine during Katharine's student days; therefore, all her published work of those years appeared in journals that reached a wide audience. Some half-dozen newspapers and religious and literary periodicals were accepting not only poems and stories, but articles of literary criticism as well. In 1879, when William Dean Howells found her poem "Sleep" worthy of publication in the *Atlantic Monthly*, her class and college felt that she had received an accolade. The final seal was set upon her happiness when Mr. Durant took the literary club, "The O. P.'s," to call upon Mr. Longfellow, who singled out Katharine to tell her that he had read the poem and had liked it.

The last year passed, less impressive in senior honors than the students anticipated. To be sure, they had a senior corridor and parlor (although it was only a section of a hall curtained with damask draperies from an '80 home and furnished with whatever could be begged from near-by '80 mothers), and they occupied the front seats in chapel. But the expected dignity and arrogance did not suddenly descend upon them, and they realized that they were, as the class historians wrote, "only Freshmen gone to seed."

Class day and commencement came and went. Each member of the class, hostess to an allotted six guests, received her diploma with a "complacent smile." But Arthur, the brother who had made all this possible for Katharine and who had so rejoiced in her progress during the four years, could not witness the exercises. Of the male sex only a parent or guardian was admitted. When Arthur learned that Mrs. Durant, indulging in special privilege, had invited several young Harvard students to be her guests, he never forgave the college.

It was one of the keenest disappointments of his life, and no words of his sister ever softened his resentment.

The class of '80 left the much-loved halls and campus with a fine reputation for scholarship and originality. Katharine, the class-day poet, wrote of them later:

This, O this, is the Classical Class,
This is the Class of '80,
Who even at play on the green young grass
Gossiped in Greek and punned—alas!
In Latin that might or might not pass.
This is that wise and weighty,
Homeric, Virgilian, Classical Class.
This is the Class of '80!

VI

"Other Days and Other Lessons"

THE STUDENT YEARS were over, and Katharine now faced the serious business of earning her daily bread. Teaching, of course, would be the means. The twenty-one-year-old girl, who had been "Kitty Cat" and "Kittie Lee" to her classmates, must now become "Miss Bates" and in her turn face a roomful of students. Until Thanksgiving she was free to rest at home and write, for until that time no offer of a position came her way. Then Natick High School, a few miles distant, employed her to teach Latin, algebra, and English, and there she gained her first experience. She refused reappointment the following autumn to accept an invitation to go to Dana Hall at Wellesley, opened that year under Julia and Sarah Eastman as a preparatory school for the college. Miss Sarah had been a member of the college, and Katharine knew and loved both women and was happy to be a part of the new school. She found Dana Hall, where she taught Greek, Latin, and geometry, "a place to love," but her scholarly standards were at variance with those of Miss Sarah and Miss Julia, and she was soon ill at ease. She planned to leave in 1883 but yielded to the sisters' entreaties because of their burden of work and remained at Dana Hall until her alma mater offered her a position three years later.

The parting came, half-reluctantly on her side, for she had many misgivings about college teaching. The head of the

English department at Wellesley, Louise Manning Hodgkins, had broached the idea of teaching there to Katharine a year before she left Dana Hall, but Katharine did not give the proposal serious consideration at the time. After accepting the Wellesley offer, she wrote Miss Hodgkins that hard work never tired her but that as a student she had observed the many emotional strains placed on the teachers and feared they were inevitable and would tell upon her.

With pride and affection the Misses Eastman released Katharine. But it was no real parting, for the women remained neighbors for many years and continued to count one another among their dearest friends. Katharine paid a guest the highest honor when she took her to call at the Eastman home. She treasured a note from Miss Sarah which read: "My dear sister, I wonder if you can know how very dear you are to me and how the very thought of you often strengthens my judgment and controls my decisions."

At Wellesley Katharine was offered a choice of work in the Greek or English departments. She chose the latter, though she shrank from the public appearances and platform addresses she knew the choice entailed. Five happy years followed, years of comparatively light responsibility when there was ample time for reading, for poetry, for friends, and for long walks about the village and the campus. Her mother and Jen were now boarding in Brighton. The boys were gone, Arthur to Portland, Maine, where his company had moved, and Sam to Philadelphia. Cornelia had given up her home so that she would be free to make long visits to her sons or to take rooms in Wellesley where she could be near her "Infant."

Katharine's pen was busy, and poems, stories, and articles followed one another rapidly. She was growing and developing, making no extravagant claims for her verses in her own mind but enjoying her ability and getting amusement and pleasure from the repercussions of her spreading reputation.

In her scrapbook she pasted one particular newspaper retort to a poem in which she had apostrophized a new gold and pearl pen:

> Katharine Bates wants to know, in a general way:—
>
> *"But how shall my song set free*
> *From the shimmering cells of my ocean pearl*
> *The music that haunts the sea?"*
>
> If you care for our advice, Katharine, we say, don't do it. Not by no manner of means. If you have the music that haunts the sea shut up in the shimmering cells of an ocean pearl, you keep it there. Don't let it out for anything. It is awful music. We heard it once when it was shut up, to a certain extent, in the shimmering cells of an after-state-room, close over the screw, and we never want to hear it again. It was dreadful. And if Katharine really has any thought of setting it free, now that she has it shut up in shimmering cells, the people who are thinking of going to Europe next summer ought to form a syndicate and buy the pearl of her, and then deposit it in a Newark bank, where nobody would ever see it again.

This type of response was as much to her taste as the many letters of appreciation from her readers. All her life she took every opportunity that offered for fun and nonsense to offset the serious business of each day. She enjoyed a joke turned against herself as well as one at another's expense—but only when the fun was kindly. Malicious wit with a sting she would have none of.

Modest though she might be about her poetry, Katharine believed that there was a place for the

> *bards who ring*
> *From door to door the little bells of Rhyme.*

Her own bells were striking ever-deepening tones as her powers grew and her understanding broadened. Her prose and poetry now appeared in magazines and journals all across the land. Her stories still drew occasionally upon Falmouth life, but she now had a wide acquaintance, and she had lived in communities where her quick perceptions brought accurate knowledge of human nature. Her critical articles showed insight, imagination, and honesty, and her poetry revealed philosophical and religious thought, although her spontaneous lyrics on nature were perhaps her happiest. The college turned to her for resolutions upon the deaths of members of the college body, and she began a series of laments and threnodies which she continued to write for many years.

In a sonnet composed at the end of her college years she had said, "There follow other days and other lessons." These days she was living joyously and absorbing the lessons eagerly, and she poured it all into her lyrics. She wrote her first poem about America at this time, already seeing it "young, eager, beautiful," and

something more
Than cloud-enfolded hills or foam-lit shore,
Or steepled towns.

She was only two years a graduate when she first wrote upon solitude, of which she was to have so little in her life of pressing tasks and crowding friendships. The sea and its transmuted imagery were in much of her work. Spring's recurring beauty and the far mysterious flights of birds were common themes. And there began to appear hints of the indomitable spirit with which she met the sorrows and disappointments of her life. She did not shrink from the difficult choice or the hard task. She already had

laughter and love and a spirit of
Unconquerable stuff,

and she knew that

hearts that turn from sorrow miss
Its hushed beatitude.

She was teaching herself to live and unconsciously, or perhaps consciously, strengthening herself for the years ahead.

Most significant were her poems of "dream and deed"—of the unseen spirit to which her life was devoted. She recognized it in her college and in her country, and it was the motive force of every act of her life—not a mere aspiration toward a goal of perfection in accomplishment, but an ideal conception toward which to strive. The heart must "out-soar the hand." She wrote in these early years "The Ideal," a poem which came to mean much to many readers and which appeared, slightly altered, in her first volume of collected poems (published when she was over fifty years old). Of its eight stanzas the first and last reveal her vision and her poetic skill:

By the promise of noon's blue splendor
in the dawn's first silvery gleam
By the song of the sea that compelleth
the path of the rock-cleaving stream,
I summon thee, recreant dreamer,
to rise and follow thy dream.

Call me thy foe in thy passion:
claim me in peace for thy friend;
Yet bethink thee by lowland and upland,
wherever thou willest to wend,
I am thine Angel of Judgment;
mine eyes thou must meet in the end.

Among the few letters that she saved was one sent to her several months after the publication of this poem:

My dear Miss Bates

Your poem the "Ideal" has come to occupy such a place in

my life that I have for some time wanted to thank you for it, to try to make you feel how it comes home to all the thinking and feeling of one who knows nothing of you and has no reason except the intrinsic worth of the poem, for feeling deeply thankful that it exists.

Every line in it is an experience of mine or has helped to create one; it rings true and pure on our deepest life and makes our hearts beat quick.

I say "our" because I have showed it to many friends in many stages of development and have found that my appreciation of it is not due to anything peculiar to my needs and experiences. It has rung in my head unexpectedly at all kinds of times, the more constantly since I have been trying to put music to it, and I would to God I could bring to you the happiness that would surely come with the sense of having done such a service to the world as your poem has done.

Graduates of Harvard especially, as in my case, that choose medicine for their life work are probably not associated in your mind with an over-expression of feelings and so I hope that you may not have to take any salt with what I say, or doubt that

I am very gratefully and sincerely yours

Richard C. Cabot

As Katharine's reputation grew, so did Wellesley's pride in her. She was looked upon as the college laureate, and praises were heaped upon her to an embarrassing degree. She received them with a secret twinkle in her eye, knowing exactly how much was sincere and honest, how much was fulsome and sentimental. Many things of an extravagant nature were said which were much to her family's distaste, accustomed as they were to plain ways and plain speech. But praise and recognition failed to turn Katharine's head. As she soberly wrote to a classmate, "I have never taken the word 'poet' to myself. I refused only last week to let myself be so catalogued in a new

'Literature.' Life calls me in too many directions. Importunate verses clamor for utterance, but usually in vain. Classes must be heard, lectures made ready, the girls' troubles listened to, the Courant [an undergraduate publication] managed, Faculty meetings attended, and miserable money earned."

The Wellesley where she now lived had become in the ten or twelve years a different college. There were new buildings, more driveways and footpaths, and the thousand rhododendrons imported by Mr. Durant were blooming yearly. The Longfellow fountain and pool lent its flash of blue to the beauty of the campus more intimately than Waban. The wooded retreat was now open to the world, and students in the ever-larger classes were less cloistered. Much as she loved the Wellesley oaks and pines, Katharine rejoiced in the growth of her college and wrote, "Let tree after tree rustle down to make room for the new buildings sealed up for us, we trust, in unsuspected wills, or, if not, clinking bravely in the slender purses of the alumnae."

One of Katharine's friends has described her in this period: "I remember the first time I ever saw her. She was crossing the first floor Centre, her arms full of books, her round head held high, her step remarkably light, and she was humming a little tuneless song. Behind those glasses that stayed on her nose as by a miracle, her eyes twinkled with the mischievous gleam we all came to know so well. Who that knew her in those vigorous days can ever forget that buoyant figure?"

These were perhaps Katharine's happiest adult years. She was still free from the many cares that were soon to multiply, and she had many friends. Colleagues and students became companions of a lifetime, for she drew people to her naturally. She had work, "but not enough." Fearing for the health of her "Head," she urged Miss Hodgkins to take a holiday and begged to be allowed to take upon her own shoulders Miss

Wellesley College in 1875

T. Lewis, Cambridgeport, Mass.

Katharine Lee Bates's room in College Hall

Hodgkins' classes. Katharine represented her offers as an opportunity to learn, and as for the students, she assured her superior that she would "handle them as if they were bubbles, —each crossed by a rainbow of literary promise." Katharine also began to think of further formal study, and an opportunity was opened for her in a most unexpected manner. During a visit to a friend and former pupil, Annie Beecher Scoville, Katharine was exposed to smallpox, and while she was in enforced quarantine in a rented room in Boston she occupied herself by writing a story for young people, *Rose and Thorn*, which she entered in a prize contest conducted by the Congregational Sunday School and Publishing Society. To her great joy she won the first prize of $700. For the first time she could think of work abroad, for Professor Eben N. Horsford of Cambridge, an old friend of Mr. Durant's and a Wellesley benefactor, invested in her, as a member of the faculty, half again the amount of her prize. A year's leave had been advised by her doctors, for severe and recurring attacks of grippe during the past two years had caused a partial breakdown of her health. With Miss Hodgkins' advice she made definite plans for study at Oxford, after which she would submit a thesis and apply for a Master's degree at Wellesley. She wrote to Miss Hodgkins in the spring while she was convalescing from another illness: "Please be thinking about my second degree. I don't care much for the letters, but I may as well do what others do, and I dislike as an A.B. to direct A.M. work. I don't care to turn aside very much from my regular line of work for it, either. Could I apply for a degree in '91 on these conditions,—major subject Elizabethan; minor subject Anglo-Saxon and Early English?"

Although she spent much of the year 1889–90 away from her classroom, Katharine carried on her work as best as she could, grateful to her colleagues and her superior for their help and understanding. She wrote to Miss Hodgkins in praise of Vida Dutton Scudder, who had taken over some of her classes: "It was exceedingly kind in Miss Scudder to read the lectures. I have always enjoyed that same sweet, fresh, helpful disposition in her, which you extol. It was the kinder in her to read the lectures, as I'm quite sure she couldn't agree with them. I told her she might be shaking her head all the time she read."

Following her occasional illnesses she was banished from time to time to near-by country towns for rest or change. Unable to be entirely idle, she wrote another story for children, *Hermit Island* (in which she used for background material a summer vacation in Arthur's cottage on the Maine coast), edited Coleridge's *Rime of the Ancient Mariner*, and compiled and edited a group of ballads which stood, eventually, in lieu of a formal thesis for her master's degree. She also began a sequel to *Rose and Thorn* and said that she was going to "try to make larger clothes for Rose and Thorn. If the needle pricks me, though, I shall throw it away. . . . I hope in the quiet year away to do at least a wee bit of writing for the truth's sake, and not for the wearisome dollar's sake. These stories are only stepping stones." Partly for that "wearisome dollar" she turned out lyrics and short stories in large quantity. She found her material all about her; even experiences and incidents of her illnesses brought grist to her mill.

But the day came when Katharine must put aside her writing, for there were plans to be made for the trip to England. Annie Scoville was to be her traveling companion. "Nannie" had been a special student at Wellesley, had taken work with Katharine in English literature, and had taught for a time at Dana Hall. She always referred to Katharine as "dear Teach." The student-teacher relationship was no barrier to friendship. Letters of excited anticipation were exchanged between the two, and at last they were actually committed to sail from a Brooklyn pier on May 22 aboard the "State of Nebraska."

VII

"Among the Heather-Bells"

NO SINGLE PERIOD of Katharine's life was more eventful or brought greater development than the years 1890–91. The great feminist movement which she had observed in her childhood days brought the first women's colleges into being and firmly established the principle that the opportunities for women should be equal to those for men. Oberlin had broken the ground as the first college to admit women and grant them the degree of Bachelor of Arts. Emma Willard, Mary Lyon, and many another in the nineteenth century had taken up the cause and had enthusiastically given their lives to the establishment of academies and seminaries, raising money, making converts, organizing, teaching, and turning their hands to all the tasks involved. With the passing of a few decades the development of public high schools enabled these pioneer schools to offer more advanced courses and attain full college status. In 1865 Vassar led the way among colleges founded exclusively for women. The interest of forward-looking men and women brought gifts and endowments, and within a few years Smith and Wellesley were also ready to absorb the ambitious young women crowding into their classrooms.

All her life Katharine Bates had been well aware of the changes and advances in the position of women, and she was always to endorse every forward step. As student, and now as educator, she took her place and assumed her share in the furthering of the educational aspects of the movement. Heretofore her adult life had been lived within comparatively narrow bounds, though students and faculty members from far and wide had put her in touch with the American world beyond New England. Until this time she had been protected and sheltered. Still under the influence of its founder, Wellesley was only slightly less secluded, and the town was a rural village with simple, neighborly ways. The formally-educated, self-reliant American woman was just beginning to emerge.

In 1890 almost any two women of thirty starting alone for Europe would have been unsophisticated and young by today's standards of maturity, and despite their intellectual backgrounds Katharine and Nan were inclined to be naïvely enthusiastic and idealistic. This was their first journey away from familiar places, and they were impatient for the experiences awaiting them when they met and mingled with colleagues from many lands.

A departure for Europe in 1890 was quite an undertaking. Advice was garnered from seasoned travelers, and clothing was planned for every possible change of temperature. Gifts ranging from the eminently practical to the bizarre were presented to the bewildered pair. Katharine must be seen off, of course, and Arthur and Sam arrived in Brooklyn from Portland and Philadelphia for the great event. Arthur wrote to his mother describing the occasion:

My dear Mother:

I have just mailed you Sife's note and a P. S. of my own. I reached N.Y. at 5.30 yesterday afternoon, took the elevated to the Battery and a ferryboat which landed me close to the State Line Pier. I traveled over the boat and after waiting half an hour saw Sam and Katharine walking on to the Pier. We found a place to leave a bag of Miss Scoville's which she was carrying and I then took her and Sam to the Mansion House—a very nice hotel—and gave them a comfortable dinner. We then went back

advice and notes of introduction, there was one she read and reread. Her mother had written several letters to be opened on successive days. This one Katharine put away carefully and kept all her life:

My dear Katie—

My hand wobbles but I will write you a little letter for Sunday. I had a Biblical riddle that I meant for a part of your Sunday employment—but many of my papers and note books were packed in the boxes that were carried into Jeannie's third story room and I could not get at them—However you will have enough to employ your thoughts and time for Sunday. By that time you will be a good sailor if you have not been one before—and will gaze with great delight and awe and peace on "this great and wide sea" I trust. I hope you may have "azure weather" and that your trip may be just restful. You can think of me as probably sitting by my window or on the piazza with thoughts that will wander off to sea, and to the precious freight it bears on its bosom. May the good ship prove to be an "Araby the Blest."

I presume you will find some congenial people, and some to whom your own sweet spirit can minister comfort and hope.

I imagine you will have divine service since we hear there is to be at least one clergyman aboard. I should think divine service at sea must be very impressive.

I am in constant remembrance of your dutiful attentions to me in a thousand ways—and wherever you are on land or sea—in this world or in another you will always be my own cherished well-beloved child, who came to me when it seemed as if life's star had set, and who has been a sunbeam always since you came. Now, brighten up, recover strength, avoid dangerous modes of traveling—enjoy all you can, have no dismal forebodings and keep your eyes steadfastly on the light ahead—and think of the joyful time when we shall meet again, dear child—

Mother—

In the few hours of fair weather and good spirits Katharine welcomed the pleasure and entertainment the trip afforded: the children, the two Englishwomen who were "nice about America," the changing skies, and the sea she had loved so long. With Nan, "the jolliest of junketers," she was determined to have a happy year. "Happiness," she wrote Miss Hodgkins, "is a part of my very small parcel of orthodoxy."

The long voyage at last drew to a close, and the travelers, shepherded by an attentive young Englishman, went ashore in an open tender at Greenock, Scotland, as the rain poured down upon them and Katharine murmured to the disconsolate Nan, " 'Jenny's a'wat, poor body. Jenny's seldom dry.' "

Worn out by her journey and her too-friendly ship acquaintances, Katharine contemplated making the homeward crossing alone on a raft so that she might look at the Atlantic and "think a thought or two." But after reaching Glasgow and the hotel, sleep and comfort restored the adventurers, and they were soon ready for a summer of wandering before the fall term at Oxford.

A few days were spared for the city before the trip to the island of Arran. After paying brief respects to some of Glasgow's buildings and monuments, they started for the cathedral, pausing on the way for milk and shortbread. Katharine wrote, "Our first cathedral stood under a smoky sky, itself dark, old, majestic, with a hill of tombs behind and flat burial slabs all about. We paid 'tuppence' each to our first beadle and entered the great nave, passing thence to choir and Lady Chapel and Chapter House and back to crypt. It strengthened all my heart to see the God-faith of the race arched and columned in such massive and enduring form, and I adopted the motto of one of the old, emblazoned coats of arms,—'*J'espère*.' I liked the starry lights in the upper windows, I liked the worn, sloping steps, I loved the brooding spirit of worship. There was hardly enough of Christ in the designs for me, and yet I found them beautiful,—and there was a lovely little Nativity window in the crypt. Nan was all for the old pagan-Scots and their coats of arms, with their devices, 'Gang forward,' 'Spare nought,' 'Ready, aye ready,' (under a window setting forth the Christian beauty of love and mercy and forgiveness) and the burgher's motto, 'Let the Deed Shaw.' " Here Katharine began her year-long communion with that "brooding spirit of worship" which she kept silently in heart and mind while outwardly she was preoccupied with all the varied beauty of the visible manifestations of the "God-faith."

But Glasgow could not hold them long. They were longing for peace and quiet and were soon off for Arran where at last Katharine began to rest and relax. Sleep, as always, continued to elude her. "Sleeping," she wrote, "is like falling in love, or saving your soul. You can't do it if you put your mind on it. It must be a divine accident. My Mother says I feel a little sleep as a horse does his oats."

In spite of the "strange bright evenings" she went to bed early every night and somehow contrived enough sleep to enjoy roaming the island with Nan, missing none of its beauty nor the ways and speech of the islanders. The new impressions were woven into poems and stories which were soon on their way back across the sea to her publishers. She had written Miss Hodgkins, "I'm glad you like 'The Ideal.' It has no lack of faults, but it stands for the order of work I want to do." But during the weeks at Arran she turned from serious ambition and wrote light, happy lyrics and a few poems for special occasions, among them a poem for a classmate's wedding:

Among the Heather-Bells

Where grey the peaks of Arran rise
To guard old Ossian's tomb,

And all the sunshine flees the skies
To blossom in the broom,
Where 'neath the drooping hawthorn sprays
The fairies loved to dance
Ere English speech and English ways
Had frighted them to France,
There one the misty mountain climbs
And loiters down the dells,
Who'll listen for your wedding chimes
Among the heather-bells.

Though songfully the silver burn
May ripple to the sea,
And rustling through the upland fern
The wild deer wander free,
Though strangely sweet the curlew's call
Shrills inland from the foam,
I'll hear no sound amid them all
But echo-bells of home.
While bridal guests their blessings bring,
On far-off Arran's fells
For me your wedding-chimes shall ring
Among the heather-bells.

The days, however, were not all lyrics and idleness. Nan's "dear Teach" held her sternly to French lessons, and Nan in turn tempted Katharine to strenuous climbs and sight-seeing excursions. Katharine found the feudalism there "but show and patchwork" and was outraged that one man should claim to own the whole beautiful island. She had decided that it would take very little of Europe to convert her to socialism. The walks and climbs were frequently interrupted as Katharine lingered to play with the children and to talk to the old people, persuading them to sing the old Gaelic songs and tell old fairy tales. Their walks were long, and Katharine often returned to their lodgings exhausted. "I was too tired to sleep much but lay awake enjoying the growing sensation of rest and dreamily remembering the wild beauty of the misty mountains and deep glen,—the dear people across the wide water, and God."

At length they left Arran to tour England and make arrangements for work at Oxford, where both Nan and Katharine would become students. Scotland came first, and they lingered in Edinburgh a month and lost their hearts to "the loveliest of cities." They went on endless excursions and enjoyed it all but grew so tired they almost quarreled because Katharine couldn't understand why Nan wanted to see the field of Bannockburn, and Nan couldn't understand why Katharine must give all their cherries away to children in the streets.

Katharine welcomed friends from Dana Hall and Wellesley who now began to turn up and indulged with them in long talks of home as they rested. Although she had decided that she was not a tourist, she continued to see the sights, doing her poet's duty by Robert Burns, visiting historic buildings and memorials to Scottish great, buying her souvenirs (among them a paperweight like one Henry Irving and Ellen Terry had bought the day before), sailing around Loch Lomond, where she found the "general effects hillside heathery, sea-gull feathery, very cold weathery," and walking through the Trossachs which, to her great surprise, she found could be toured in ten minutes.

The days were filled with expeditions, studies, and friends. Katharine read and studied architectural books in preparation for her visits to the cathedrals, while Nan, the historian, was deep in Scottish and English history and the novels of Sir Walter Scott. And there were letters to be written. Katharine sat up late at night writing to her mother, careful not to omit a detail whereby she might share with her family as much as possible of her adventure. She even reported on the state of her wardrobe, always to her the most uninteresting of subjects: "I have just two suits with me, the green dress, wrap and hat, and black dress, sacque and hat. The green hat I use as a bonnet and that suit is the more elegant,—reserved for church, dignified afternoon walks and so forth. The black hat I got in Edinburgh,—nice straw, trimmed with black silk ribbon,—a small English sailor hat—shades my face,—cost, making, materials and all, five shillings."

Eventually, Katharine and Nan began to think of England, London, Oxford, and the thirty-mile walking tour they had planned from Clovelly to Wells. Though Scotland had indeed been "bonny," England was to be "home." At length the day came when they packed their bags and crossed the border.

VIII

"—*Unless Love Is*"

A WEEK was allowed for the journey to London, and a week for the cathedrals, far too little time for Katharine, who was keeping her private vigils within each "great centuried Prayer in Stone." They lingered as long as possible at Durham, York, Lincoln, and Ely, and ended their trip at Cambridge.

In London, Katharine indulged her "bookworm heart" at the British Museum and took time to look up the family name, after which she wrote her mother: "It has room for a large number of grandfather Bates' discourses, one or two pamphlets by Uncle Joshua, Uncle Sam and Aunt Mary, and even 'Rose and Thorn,' published by Nelson and Sons, of London, in a gorgeous binding of lavender, with green-leaved, very red roses running all over it, inscribed on the outside: A Story for Boys and, within, A Tale for the Young. My name is brilliantly printed on the cover, but no credit is given to the Congregational Publishing Society, or to America."

London was hot and noisy, and Katharine and Nan soon went on to Oxford where they made academic arrangements and engaged lodgings for the autumn term which was to begin in October. When these details were completed they were off again for more sight-seeing.

In all Katharine's plans for letters, poems, stories, articles, study, and sight-seeing, she allowed time for yet another endeavor. Her mother, her friends, or her own conscientious nature, or perhaps all three, had stirred her to feel that she must resolve her religious thinking and arrive at some definite belief. She was not a member of any denomination, for she had never felt drawn to a creed and had remained outside the Congregational fold of her parents. Among her friends were several confirmed Episcopalians whose beliefs she respected and considered thoughtfully. Two of the friends, Katharine Coman and Vida Scudder, both teachers at Wellesley, compiled a list of suggested readings—a somewhat dismaying list for an already too crowded summer vacation.

Before Katharine sailed for Europe she had written to a former classmate: "I live under a fatality of dumbness, or, at the least, stammering. Nothing in me, body or mind, seems plastic to my real self. I get so weary of these other shifting selves,—more angry with them than my severest judge can be. But while I protest against no judgment, wondering that any one ever catches glimpses of my actual heart under all these ugly veils, I must still state that I find no change at the centre of my spirit since the day I entered college until now. I am supposed to have become a Christian since. It seems to me that I have only learned to call by its right name the God-craving that was always there and to put it a little more into words and deeds and—silences. . . . I trust myself,—not my looks or speech or demeanour, not my 'poems' or teaching in class-room,—I am always conscious of trying, trying, trying and trying in vain to *melt* my stubborn members, physical and mental, into the truth of my soul, but still I trust the poor, dumb, hidden self which dwells in solitude and looks to God. It abides in pitiful darkness, but its entreaty is Godward. If this is not true, then there is no truth possible to me. . . . You are right in feeling that with the sense of one true service rendered, one's own poor life becomes blessed and almost glorified. Under all my own errors—and it seems as if no one ever made so many as I have managed to jumble into these thirty-one years—I have an ever-growing consciousness of the beauty—the ineffable beauty and splendor of God's work for the world and in the world. It is bitterness itself to know that I mar and hinder that work, and the very sweetness of life whenever I seem, however so little, to help."

During the year abroad she occasionally discussed the question of religious doctrine with Nan, who looked with a certain disfavor on Katharine's attendance at services of the Church of England and felt, when she herself attended, that she had not been to "meeting." It was to Katharine Coman, her closest and dearest friend throughout her life, that Katharine wrote most fully and frankly, confiding the discouragements, hopes, and disappointments that absorbed her mind and heart as she wandered with Nan on the Clovelly beaches or the moors of Devon.

Meanwhile, she conscientiously tackled the suggested readings and reported occasionally to Katharine: "Clement I feel and, in a sense, believe, but Origen's doctrine of 'the eternal generation of the Son' and the Athanasian device of 'Trinity' do not, as Coleridge would say, 'find me.' . . . I think, with you, that revelation is a consequence of the personality of God but does that mean more than that a Great Heart of Love in the universe must throb all life closer and closer to itself? I'm sure there must be a God only as thirst is sure there must be water—but there is revelation even in that, isn't there? I must read. I must read. 'Religion,' as the Frenchman said, 'is a great subject.' But I don't altogether want to read. I would rather watch the clouds and listen to the birds. Your love is a proof of God. How does love come, unless Love is? . . . That is a glorious sentence from the 'Imitation' wherewith you close your letter. I love it and I love you and I love what shadowy hint of God comes to me and long for the clearer heart that would admit a clearer light. . . . I used to long for truth as something apart and beyond,—something that could be written in a sentence or spoken in a word. But I grow more and more to feel that, until there is truth in soul and life, there can be little chance of achieving truth of doctrine. And it is hard to have the outward a clear reflection of the inward,—hardest of all to keep the spirit true. There are always so many undercurrents of perception and reflection, thought criticising thought and feeling doubting feeling. Nothing puzzles me more than this many-foldedness. I have been trying all my life to find out which I is I, and I don't know yet."

But earnest though she might be, Katharine was tired. She wrote one of her friends that she had strengthened all her faith in all good hope and exclaimed, with a hint of impatience, "I am not sure that beginners are best helped in spiritual life by having the advanced and differing spiritual experiences of others pressed upon them."

Katharine had been amused at one interpretation of her surname in its early spelling "Bate," which defined its meaning as "contentious." She was to contend for what she believed to be right on many an occasion, but now she longed to put all argument from her and be idle with Nan, discovering England through its "ghosts of kings, prelates, witches, peasants and rebels." Nan gave her time chiefly to historical monuments and remains, while Katharine devoted hers largely to churches and cathedrals, discovered unexpected pleasures in the picture galleries, and loitered about watching street fights and Punch-and-Judy shows and talking to shopkeepers, landladies, and children.

Yet she was deeply in earnest about her theological studies and pursued them faithfully throughout her entire year in Europe. She was profoundly troubled and sometimes felt that there must be some weakness within her that prevented her from saying, with her friends, "I believe." She spent long hours alone, musing on Katharine Coman's letters and on the centuries-old faiths whose relics and monuments were all around her. She loved the symbolism of the great cathedrals and the intimate wayside crosses. Of the latter she wrote, "No other human symbol stands for so many and so noble thoughts."

From her soul-searchings emerged Katharine's individual Trinity: "Christ," "Love," and "God." She found her assurance in the "shining track through the darkness," in the love of her friends, and in her instinct for worship of "Him on Whom my longings wait."

IX

"J'espère"

CLOVELLY was now the objective of the travelers. They stopped on the way at Salisbury and at Bemerton to see George Herbert's ivy-covered church. To Katharine's sorrow they were joined there by a loquacious English couple, so she had no opportunity for a quiet communion in the holy place of one of her favorite English poets.

Evading the suggestion of their English companions that they join forces for Stonehenge, they set off the next day in a dogcart behind a small pony driven by Nan. They were disappointed to find Stonehenge a noisy picnic site. But there was the "low, soft-blue English sky and over all towered the giant stones," and Katharine decided that "merry-making, after all, is better worship than human sacrifice."

Stonehenge ended the sight-seeing for a time. With no more interruption they went on to Clovelly, riding on top of the coach, where a hornet stung Nan and a low-hanging branch swept Katharine's glasses off to destruction. But home-like rooms and the best of landladies, a Mrs. Moss, awaited them. They were soon comfortably settled, in spite of the one drawback—the fleas they often encountered in their inexpensive lodgings. To Katharine's mild criticism Mrs. Moss replied, "Oh! but little clean English fleas! They can't be anything to the vermin that everybody says over-run America!"

On August 12 Katharine wrote in her journal: "My birthday. Thirty and one years behind me. Before me—what? God be thanked for the past and trusted for the future. An affectionate flea bit my toes in birthday greeting. I found my plate adorned with flowers and vines and mysterious packages,—cheese and crackers, favorite dainties of mine, being kindly presented by the House Purse, while photographs of Clovelly and squares of sweet chocolate came from Nannie-ka-chee herself. It was a beautiful day, and I had had a better rest than usual, and I knew that way across the ocean, my mother was remembering me."

Reading Kingsley, strolling with Nan, or gossiping with their kind landlady, Katharine, who was always happiest by the sea, began to build up the reserve she needed as she alternated her long walks with what were, for her, lazy days. She happily ate roast duck and Devonshire junket, lay in the heather listening to Nan read aloud, and went with her to Evensong in the little church where Kingsley's father had preached. They watched the fishing boats, picked up the banded and mottled pebbles on the beaches, and delighted in the varying colors of the bay. Katharine sent her mother lists of the flowering vines and bushes, the fuschias, geraniums, high-bush blackberries, and honeysuckle. She added a note about her wardrobe: "I took an ingenious hem all around the bottom of my black over-skirt, which at once shortens it and hides the frayed edges. Nan says it is not the proper thing to do, but it looks all right and I am proud of it."

When their time was up, the friends left Clovelly and went to Ilfracombe, the starting point for the long walk up the south coast of the Bristol Channel. They became veritable gypsies, carried packs on their backs, and took their chances on each night's lodging. They lost their way, followed inviting rivers, scrambled up and down the cliff paths, looked at Shelley's cottage, close by the sea at Lynmouth, and thought it a "beautiful place and even worthy of him." Near Exmoor they stopped for lunch at a cottage. "A kindly English dame bustled about and set out for us all the dainties of her cupboard,—heather honey and jellies and clotted cream, all arranged about the 'cold shoulder,' which an Exmoor sheep turned to us. And while we unstrapped our bags and feasted, she discovered that we were Americans and begged leave to bring in two young gentlemen, lodgers of hers, because one of them had a sister in California and another in Africa and she seemed to think that we should all have a savage joy in meeting."

Fortified against hunger and armed with a compass, they were soon on the open moor, too happy to fear becoming lost. "On all sides was nothing but the rolling purple moor,—one purple flush of heather, and the sky almost touching earth." Their compass led them accurately to the cottage where they were to spend the night, and the next day, in spite of heavy rain, Nan's heart was so set on seeing the Doone Valley that they pushed on, taking shelter in a shepherd's hut during the worst downpour. There they found "two dandy sportsmen, waiting, all booted and spurred and with their horses in the shed, for the hunt to sweep that way and give them a chance to fall in. One of these white-trousered youths assured us that the house he occupied still bore on its heavy oak door the marks of the robbers' blows and contained a secret chamber and outlet, for protection from them. Nan believed him, every word, but I eyed him critically and, since he had just returned from a trip to America, I fear much that he had learned to lie."

The trip ended that day at Malmsmead, after thirty-five miles of walking. Here, muddy and wet through, they climbed into a wagon and were driven into Minehead where they took the train to Taunton. They found a comfortable hotel and "a gorgeous apartment with a rocking chair on a dais. We were both so tired that, while we were waiting for supper, we sat together in the one chair on the proud dais and feebly crooned

Sunday-School hymns, till we were afraid the chambermaid might listen at the keyhole and take us for a Dissenting prayer-meeting."

All along the way Katharine amused herself by observing those who bore her name: the William Bates whose name led a list of those who had not paid their taxes, and the amiable lunatic named Kate Bates who had occupied a cottage at Clovelly.

The strenuous part of the summer was over and the friends went on through Glastonbury to Wells where they separated, Nan to join other companions until they met at Oxford, and Katharine, who took naturally to solitude, to continue her leisurely way, lingering here and there as she pleased.

As she went from cathedral to cathedral, musing on the faith of the generations of worshipers, she read theological books, in particular *The Continuity of Christian Thought* by Alexander V. G. Allen. She spent rainy mornings in her lodgings, pondering the old doctrines and trying to resolve them, yet knowing that she must find truth, which would not be written between the covers of a book, but, uninterpreted by any oracle, would speak to her listening heart. It was a happy religion, this evolving faith of Katharine's, and it was the only one possible to her. She looked at her truths squarely and found in her constant realization of the Divine that she could, with honor, admit only her own experience. There was a presumption, a too-easy familiarity, in the way the theologians spoke of God. Such intimacy, such arrogation of authority to interpret, repelled her. But the search in each man's heart, the longing, the "hope of God" which she later wrote that she chose to serve, these she understood and these were her own.

Strength came gradually but surely. Before she returned to Wellesley, her goal had been reached. She was content with the knowledge that her spiritual life must be one long seeking, without personal revelation. She had chosen truly when she took as her motto *J'espère.*

Katharine went slowly on to Stratford, absorbing eagerly all that came to her attention, writing in her journal minute details of cathedral and parish-church architecture, and noting always the ways and speech of the people and the flowers in the gardens and along the wayside. She stood in Bristol upon the unconsecrated ground before Thomas Chatterton's monument and noticed with annoyance the basket of market vegetables beside it, the broken glass and bits of coal scattered upon its base. For Nan's sake she visited historic castles, happiest when their picture galleries were open, and said in her journal, "For the first time in my life I wish I were on visiting terms with the English nobles. I want to see their pictures."

During a day spent in Wales at Llandaff she saw, in one sense, her best cathedral, for "the beautiful thing about the whole is that this generation of people have labored, lovingly and zealously, to restore their old cathedral, and it has the democratic rather than the aristocratic look. The men who worship in it are, from Bishop to organ-blower, the men who have labored in it, with head or hands or both."

A note from Nan arrived with the news that she could meet Katharine at Oxford a week earlier than planned, so she hurried on, writing her mother from Tintern: "England is a goodly land, but sopping wet. We have had rain in this Happy Valley six days out of the last seven,—not continuous downpour, but the valley is swathed in heavy mist and at any moment water falls. Such weather damps my tourist enthusiasm and I lie on the sofa and read novels and amuse myself by saucing their sacred climate to my horrified yet apologetic landlady. That a savage American should presume to make fun of any thing English! And yet a lodger who readeth books must be treated with respect. When I happen upon the more intelligent English people, they try to conceal their compassion for one born outside the hallowed circle of their fogs and usually ask me if I *intend to return* to America. Yesterday a lady asked me if we had any hills and if South America was pretty. And at the entrance of a park,—a city park, not private—I usually encounter the British lion in bronze, nonchalantly rolling the round world under his paw. On the other hand, I do come across plenty of loud-voiced, ungrammatical, flashy Americans, and have to admit that Uncle Sam has still many things, especially in the way of courteous bearing and refined address, to teach his perky children. English children,—among the gentry, at least—are better mannered than our own little Democrats. If a small boy stumbles against me in a race, he falls out of line to come back and lift his solemn little hat and say, 'I beg your pardon.' Small boys in England are very jolly altogether,—sturdy, red-cheeked, fisticuffing and tumbling continually, but quiet and good-natured with it all, and amazingly good to the babies. . . . The chief drawback to my happiness in my lodgings is a case of stuffed birds, tho' I've no consistent right to object to that, when I don't object (and yet in heart I do) to the stuffed bird I often see on my platter. . . . I have paid three visits to the Abbey, one in sunshine, one in mist and one in moonlight. It is beautiful for situation, in this narrow valley of the Wye, with the green hills looking in at the mullioned windows and the graceful arches tapestried with woodbine and ivy. It is unroofed, with columns broken and statues lost. Grass grows on the top of the walls, an army of noisy jackdaws nest in the crevices, rising like a black cloud when one enters and saluting with hoarse screams, and the tamest, dearest little English robins, such tiny birds, with red breasts brighter than those of their big American namesakes, are perched all about on the fallen stones and broken pillars, singing away more sweetly than ever the old monks did. An excursion party was here last night to see it by moonlight,—brass band and merry-go-round and general unholy slambang. I should have thought the remaining walls of the Abbey would tumble down on their impertinent heads."

She ended her solitary journey with an afternoon at the horse races in Warwick, "to enlarge my experience of life." She apologized to England for her remarks about the weather, for there came "one of those beautiful English blue days for which it takes so many grey days to make ready," and she went on to Stratford, her last shrine on the way to Oxford and Nan. "Stratford! I meant to go alone, but fell in with two New York women on the train and had their company on the visit to Shakespeare's house, the stroll past the old Hostelry and Grammar School and the visit to the church. Everything was just as I had always known it would be, and there was, as I expected, little enough of the spirit-Shakespeare there. The ashes of his body,—what are they beside the living fire of his soul, still burning his words upon the heart and conscience of the two great hemispheres?" Shottery, the birthplace of Anne Hathaway, was "just what the books have always told,—what I have always known."

Katharine closed her travel journal: "To Oxford, and to Nan, and in a new volume the new life, student's not tourist's must begin."

X

Oxford

KATHARINE was to go abroad many times, always with enlarged capacities for absorbing foreign cultures and with ever wider sympathy and understanding. But on later journeys she was a mature woman, her character formed and her beliefs resolved. Aware that her first trip abroad would prove a crossroads in her life, Katharine kept a complete journal during this time, a record of her study and travels and the events which determined finally her modes of thought and the direction of her life. No later journal was given such painstaking care.

In the first days at Oxford, she wrote and dispatched voluminous letters home, and she found time to conclude the search for books on organ-building for her brother Sam and to send off the poems and stories she had written during the summer. She also made agreements to write several articles based on her study at Oxford. She could no longer say, as she had to one correspondent who had reproached her for not writing, "If I am cross, I say to my conscience that such is the natural and wholesome expression of wearied nerves. If I am lazy, I say how virtuous it is in me to rest. If I neglect all my correspondents, I think complacently how happy my self-denying friends must be in this marked indication that I am foregoing human labors."

Katharine settled down with Nan in their Oxford lodgings and made the first entry in her journal:

Oct. 9, To turn from gypsy life to the respectabilities requires some attention to the outside of the platter. Nan was already gloriously adorned, and I bought hat and sacque and a beauteous umbrella and sent my ulster and old sacque to a job-tailor's to be rejuvenated. We marketed, worked a little at the unpacking and arranging, and then Nan nestled her aching head against me, while we watched the sunset amber in the sky opposite our parlor window. 'Tis so good to have her again. We have started out on a rigorously healthful diet, with French for supper, and hope to begin our architectural rambles soon. I sat up later than she did tonight, and our little maid, Rose, bro't me six letters, which made me both sad and glad, thoughtful and wistful, and dangerously like homesick.

A few passages from one of her first letters to her family describe her life:

We are really snuggled at last under the outermost wing feathers of this ancient bird of learning and are given to understand that she will peck us pretty smartly if we do not acquit ourselves with such credit as semi-civilized Americans can. . . . Saturday morning we were invited to seek the presence of Mrs. Johnson and present our schedules. She is of the angular type of English woman, very straightforward, very breezy. On the street you see nothing of her house but an ugly wall with curtained windows and a door with a grim knocker. Within you enter a large hall, on one side a gentleman's study, books and whips, manuscripts and guns in about equal proportion, and on the other side a long drawing-room, with comparatively little furniture, all choice, and opening out upon a beautiful flower-garden. In the middle of her talk with us she had to rush away to drag her dog out of a dog-fight on the street. Nan says sadly that she never tried to do anything in England yet but she was interrupted by a dog-fight. Mrs. Johnson solemnly registered us as students under the Oxford Association for the Collegiate Education of Women,—whereupon, in excess of joy, we paid down five shillings apiece. She bade us hasten to join the Debating Society and under her direction we meekly sent one shilling apiece to Miss Rogers, of Greek renown, who responded that we were enrolled as members and that she would come to call upon us, if there was not illness in her home. We were also sent to the Bodleian to get "forms" for the reading privilege and the porter insisted that we wanted to go up on the roof, which we didn't at all, and made us pay our threepences for "the view, ladies, the view," before he would show us the librarian's desk. . . . There's an "American Fair" going on here. People bring their old clothes to exchange for pots and pans and then the clothes are given to the poor. I'm told it is a common form of American charity.

Oxford was all that she had dreamed, and she could have spent days roaming through the buildings and quads and exploring the countryside and the neighboring villages. It was for her, as for Matthew Arnold, the city that, "spreading her gardens to the moonlight, and whispering from her towers the last enchantments of the middle ages . . . by her ineffable charm, keeps ever calling us nearer to the true goal of all of us, to the ideal, to perfection, to beauty, in a word, which is only truth seen from another side." She was tempted to loiter by "the lovely old gardens, shadowed by the grey walls and autumn-wan with poplars and aspens, chestnuts and elms, all yellow and drifty and quiet, yet with bright borders of single and double dahlias." She stole time for a walk along the tow-path to Iffley to see its Norman church, and she turned with equal pleasure from the "misty, many-towered landscape" to watch the crews in training for the spring races. At Oxford she saw "Addison's Walk," which she described to her mother: "In this famous walk, which in the spring will be bordered by blue myrtle, we two humblest spirits of the New World came upon the reverend Vice-Chancellor himself, walking between two Fellows, three gowned, monastic figures that paced with slow and solemn tread."

But the lectures, and the men who gave them, were of first importance, and she tried to make her family see her teachers as she did:

> The redoubtable Dr. Wright, a short, ruddy man, who prides himself, and with justice, on his philology. He hates American students, especially women, and says they have no ability, anyway, only a little shallow enthusiasm. . . . Prof. Napier, who gesticulates by nervous little pulls at his auburn mustache. . . . Prof. Earle, a fine picture of the scholar, in his black silk gown, with his white hair, and refined, thin, mind-lit old face. . . . the lecturer [unnamed], a very soulful young man, wrapped his sable robe about him and paced up and down before his audience of admiring girls, as he discoursed, with a sad, monotonous motion. But his points were clearly, tersely and delicately made, and for matter it was in the pure Oxford strain, much about Man, and God and Nature and a little about Wordsworth.

The lecturer on Spenser was a disappointment—"a young, nervous, bashful boy who had 'got it up.' " The lecturers for the Association were all somewhat disappointing, in no way to be compared to the regular University lecturers.

Since the shy young lecturer on Spenser had little to impart, Katharine dropped his course, as well as Dr. Wright's, who had been trained in the German philological school and cared nothing for his texts as poetry or literature or even as sentences. The roots of the words were his only concern. He growled at Katharine, "Poets,—why they don't even know the meaning of the words they use." He had, once upon a time, read and even written poetry, but now it was all "pure ignorance," and, according to Katharine, a page of the dictionary was more to his taste.

Most interesting of all were the famous men whom they were occasionally able to hear, and Katharine wrote of them while her impressions were fresh:

The event of Monday was a lecture by Walter Pater, "Fellow of Brasenose and Apostle of the Renaissance." I had a lecture the hour before and when I arrived at Mr. Pater's lecture-room, I found it overflowing into vestibule, down steps and into the street. Many of the crowd went away, but I didn't, and inch by inch was shoved toward the door. I certainly came "into contact" with the English people for once. By the time the lecture was a quarter over, I was across the threshold,—by the time it was half over, I had caught several polished sentences,—by the time it was three quarters over, I had intermittent glimpses, between the heads of tall young Oxonians, of a bald, middle-aged forehead and a black moustache,—and by the time it was all over, I had a seat.

Thursday afternoon the Oxford Professor of Poetry,—a title once borne by Matthew Arnold,—gave the first of the three lectures which he is bound to deliver in the course of a year. He's a little, ruddy man, said to be somewhat Browningesque in look, who walked in before his audience of about fifty, mostly ladies, in all the glory of his Master of Arts gown,—black, the deep hood lined with red and bro't around like a sailor-collar in front and piped with red. Did I say he was Palgrave, the compiler of the Golden Treasury, something of a critic, and something less of a poet, and one of the few intimates of Tennyson? His lecture was on Surrey, excellent in substance, of course, but very badly given, the lecturer sitting down, burying his head in his manuscript and reading as fast as he could, as if he were anxious to have an unpleasant task over with. Twice he glanced up to remark: "As Tennyson once said to me" etc. He lectured again Friday, standing to his work, this time, and doing it much better. He has a pleasant look, bright eyes and a good forehead. . . . We went to hear Augustine Birrell at the Russell Club, a middle-aged, square-headed, black-haired, side-whiskered, twinkling-eyed gentleman whose address was running over with wit and thought and literature.

One of Katharine's earliest and most lasting impressions was of the famous Dr. Murray. Her encounter with him was somewhat painful:

Miss Whedon took us to see Dr. Murray's Dictionary. That is one of the sights of Oxford. Dr. Murray, who had met Miss Whedon and, knowing we were from Wellesley, asked her to bring us, is an old, old, very nice gentleman, with benevolent face and flowing, snow-white beard. The University has engaged him to write a dictionary that shall be worthy of the attention of the enlightened English people. Common dictionaries they scorn. There is nothing that seems to amuse an Englishman who has been in America more than the fact that every house has a dictionary and the inmates fly to it as an authority. They have no such arbitrary standards, bless 'em! They pronounce as it seems good to their own educated souls and look on us with kindly compassion because we don't say "figgers" and "diffi'kulty" and "been" (like bean). In that last point I dare say they have the better of us. But Dr. Murray is making and has for many years been making, with a large staff of assistants, a mammoth dictionary, which shall be in many volumes and give fullest etymology and history of every word, with copious illustrations in chronological order. *They are working on C.* This Herculean labor is carried on by gaslight in a long, low narrow room, without windows, the walls lined with cubby-holes full of papers. The Clarendon Press has offered him large, well-lighted and well-ventilated rooms, but he clings to his little den, tho' many of his workers sicken and have to leave him. Hereby hangs a tale—a melancholy tale—for I still bear a trace of my last winter's illness, a tendency, unknown before, to turn faint on slight provocation.

Well! we entered Dr. Murray's sanctum late in the afternoon, and the air was almost unbreathable. He very courteously began an explanation of the whole long process. I was vastly interested at first, then I became aware, to my horror, that his voice was getting further and further away and the room was turning black and beginning to swim. I clutched the table and held out a moment or two longer, thinking how awfully illiterate it would look to the English mind if an American should faint away at the mere sight of his dictionary,—but it was no use. I had to make a hurried excuse and just succeeded in getting to the door, where the open air, fog and all, was blessedness. The assistants sprang for a chair and a glass of water and the like with very suspicious alacrity, and I've since been told that nothing pleases them so much as to have a lady turn faint in their dreadful little prison-hole, since it is a living argument against non-ventilation. But Dr. Murray, tho' I returned in a few minutes, regarded me with sorrowful disapproval and cut his explanations short—which was just as well, for Nan was getting ready to take her turn at faintness. But we went down town in the tram, had hot cocoa and buns at a pastrycook's, felt revived and went to Magdalen chapel for evensong, where the anthem was the resonant old Latin hymn—Dies Irae.

Despite her enthusiasm for Oxford, Katharine had dreaded the inevitable social life and the surrendering of her solitude into which she had admitted briefly only chance acquaintances or passers-by. Now she wrote to a friend, "It's the talk for talk's sake that puts me out of patience. I don't think any vestibules, human, or inhuman, are interesting . . . People as people only interrupt and keep one from living. Friends give life and give it more abundantly."

But the social activity at Oxford could not be avoided. The

English were cordial and hospitable, and Katharine and Nan soon found themselves quite unable to accept all the invitations. As for the American students, "thro' Wellesley ramifications, or thro' Nan's grandfather [Henry Ward Beecher] or thro' my unhappy scribblings, they all have some special claim to our acquaintance. So we are going to be 'at home' every Tuesday afternoon between four and six to give them a chance to rally round Nan's diminutive flag." English friends came, too, and called the little sitting room in Walton Street "the Americans' Happy Hunting Ground." There were not hours enough in the day for the university buildings, the lectures, the friends, the countryside, the reading, the letters, and the poems and stories that Katharine still tried to write for the much-needed checks they brought. Above all, there were not hours enough for the Bodleian. But she gained a little time by dropping the debating society, whose discussions the young American bluestocking found "shallow, evasive, rambling, flippant."

Among their new American friends were several young men, who were soon escorting Katharine about and arriving to spend all her so-called "free" evenings with her. She identified them to her mother as "my Michigan brother, my Minnesota brother, my New York brother," and so on. She wrote a very interested sister Jen not to worry, for she liked them all. There were Englishmen, too, among her friends—one a young tutor who took as much of her time as she would allow and whose mother became her friend and admirer.

It was inevitable that Katharine should attract the attention of her "brothers." Her conversation was intelligent, and her original turn of wit was always at her command. She had a charming courtesy of manner, and her sympathy and interest were generous and spontaneous. In appearance she was erect, not slender, and yet not stout, as she was to be later in life. Her oval face, framed in soft brown hair, was expressive and

College Hall from Lake Waban

Wellesley College Library

Wellesley College Today

lit always by her most memorable feature, her unusually bright eyes, with their direct and trusting look.

But all the kind young Oxford friends disappeared from her story, for when their letters, and they themselves, pursued her to London and the Continent, she wrote her mother, "I sternly nip these frivolities in the bud." At Oxford, however, they were pleasant and interesting companions, and the young English tutor made himself a delightful and dependable guide to the colleges and to the countryside.

XI

The Continent

DURING all the latter part of the term a shadow had been gathering over Katharine's future. For Nan's sake she had tried to put aside the problem that letters from her friend and former classmate, Marion Pelton (now Mrs. George K. Guild), had presented to her. Mrs. Guild was Wellesley's first alumna trustee and was in a position to keep Katharine informed about the hard decision she might be called upon to make. By December she felt that she must let her mother know the situation as it stood:

I hope you will not feel disappointed or troubled to know that I seriously contemplate breaking my connection with Wellesley. The immediate reason is the pending decision of the Trustees to make a theological requirement of the teachers, and I think that will be a mistake. I cannot bind my own beliefs and I do not think it right for a college which is established to seek truth, to dictate its truth at the outset. If I decide to send in my resignation, which will not be for some weeks yet, I shall come home in the spring and try to get some sort of steady literary work. I have spent almost all my adult life in the village of Wellesley,—and I am very tired of girl-problems and girl-judgments. I do not think I could maintain my health there many months, for girls here in Oxford (always excepting Nan) tire me more than anything else. I hope you will not be sorry about this. I am almost sure such a change would be best for me in every way. I will write of it again.

During the Christmas season Katharine had a letter from Miss Hodgkins which reached her at London where she and Nan had gone for the holidays before a short trip to the Continent. She hastened to write her mother further:

I have been in twenty minds about going on the Continent at all, under these altered circumstances in regard to Wellesley. And that situation, dear Mamma, is something I want you to understand. I really think the theological points involved need not grieve you. I have no sympathy with materialistic Unitarianism. I believe Christ is divine but I never could take in doctrinal religion very easily or very fast. On most points of church belief I have to wait and learn. It would not be right or possible for me to hurry my convictions. They must have time to grow, and within the last fifteen years I think they have been steadily growing toward a deeper and more earnest faith in the essentials of the Christian religion. But the whole tendency of the college to insist on opinion rather than conduct I have always disapproved, and now that the Trustees propose to emphasize that tendency, I propose to withdraw and put my life where it can work more frankly and freely. Miss Hodgkins has written me an intolerable letter, saying that she is ready to give up the Department to me on condition that I assure her that I have a hold on "the eternal verities" and will maintain the divinity of Christ. I do accept the divinity of Christ and I trust I have some hold on the truth of life, but I should feel degraded, from the tone of her letter, to seem to buy the Department by theological pledges. If Wellesley cannot tell from my life and teaching of the past years whether I am a Christian or not, I do not find it in me to make lip-protestations, especially when there is a Professorship to be gained by it. I feel that I should be making the most sacred things of life sordid. In fact, I am hurt in no small degree, and would rather earn my livelihood by any honest means than return, after Miss Hodgkins' letter, to the College. I sent a portion of her letter to

Marion and will ask Marion to save it for you, if you want to see it. I think you would better not.

The outlook, I hope, will not depress you, either. I can surely get some teaching to do, at the worst, and probably a position very nearly equal, in salary at least, to Wellesley, and possibly the ever-coveted opportunity to maintain myself by some occupation which, less taxing than teaching, leaves strength and time for literary work. I can never do good work in writing otherwise.

If I were alone, I should go into some quiet corner now and write another story, but Nan is eager for the Continent, we are close by, as we may never be again, and less than $80.00 (only twice my last check from the Companion) will pay our ticket expenses from London through Holland, Belgium, Germany, Italy and France. . . . I am very well again, tho' I was naturally tired at the end of the Oxford term. But London, instead of distressing me by its noise and hurry, as it did in the summer, only entertains and exhilarates me. I sleep and eat, and expect to come back, perhaps in April, all right. I would rather stay longer, if I can, but if there is any work to be had, I shall come home to it, for I am anxious to pay back Professor Horsford his $300.00, which he invested in me for the College, as soon as possible. I shall not send in my formal resignation until February, which will give me time to hear from you.

After dispatching this letter Katharine received "a very pleasant letter" from Miss Hodgkins which made no reference to the matter causing Katharine so much distress of mind. In this letter she brought up the question of Katharine's second degree and asked whether Katharine would object if Miss Hodgkins requested it for her on the basis of the original work she had published, especially her poetry and articles written during the year at Oxford. So a hurried note was sent off to Katharine's mother on the heels of the previous letter:

I am afraid my last may have stirred your indignation against Miss Hodgkins, and as this note from her, read tonight, says you are to spend January 19 with her, I hasten to present her in her better light. Still, not a dozen M.A.'s comforts me for being questioned as to my theological fitness to teach literature at Wellesley. Miss Hodgkins may consider it a trifle to tell me that she has decided, after these five years, that I have "no hold on the eternal verities," but *I* don't. Every day increases my feeling that I have lived in Wellesley long enough. I shall never succeed as a writer, if I return to that narrow, absorbing, timid, nerve-wearing life. And yet I love Wellesley more than ever. Dearest Mother, please don't worry about me or my fortunes or my theology, which are all, in spite of adverse appearances, in a very fair way.

A day or so later she wrote again:

You see from my still remaining here that I am puzzled as to what I ought to do next. I think now of retiring to Canterbury for a week, out of these abominable fogs, and there deciding, but if nothing turns up to prevent, we shall probably go almost directly to Italy and settle down there quietly. I expect the next few months to be trying, but things will turn out for the best in the end. If you are not displeased or distressed, my greatest anxiety will be lifted. But you wouldn't want me to pay a pennyworth of conscience for pounds of salary and dignity, would you?

From Canterbury she wrote:

I shall be back very soon now, well and happy, to see what God wants of me next. I hope you're not distressing yourself over the Wellesley matter. It's a pity but I felt that the only fitting thing for me to do was to withdraw and leave Miss Hodgkins free to nominate a successor in whom she had confidence. . . . I've had another cheery note from her suggesting that it would be such a good thing if I could only drop teaching at once and devote myself to juvenile literature. And I've had a very friendly letter from Miss Stratton expressing her willingness to give a second degree on my published work. But I don't take to that suggestion, especially at this time.

And again from Paris where she and Nan began a short Continental tour:

I am very glad that you are not utterly distressed by this Wellesley complication. I shall not act hastily. I only want to do right in the matter, but while, as you all say, Miss H– has not the authority to reject me, I should not wish to urge my desires against a criticism like that made by one in her official position. I have a flood of protesting and sympathetic letters. Meanwhile I can't decide at all whether to go to Italy or not.

But good news came from Wellesley after all. In the hurry of her travels, Katharine wrote only a line or two, since she knew that Mrs. Guild would tell her mother the details:

As for Wellesley, the situation has changed in that the Trustees rejected, after all, the theological amendment, and passed one requiring only "Christian character." I don't know more about it until I get my letters in London, some ten days hence,—Marion cabled so much—and consequently cannot tell at all as yet what my own action must be. I will do the wisest and rightest I can.

Some weeks later she wrote at length to Katharine Coman describing her position:

Now let's see if I can make it all clear,—only promising that I probably shall go back to Wellesley, if I am well enough.

I love Wellesley—love her so much more than ever now that

she is *right*—and I think work at Wellesley as urgent and rich and noble as work anywhere in the world. Still, there is such a thing, with no disrespect to a square hole, as its not fitting a round peg, and when I am most a Wellesley teacher I always feel least myself. I think I should make a horribly bad professor—honestly I do. I can't speak well, I dread to face even a class audience, I'm sinfully bored by critical works on literature, I would like to hold my peace instead of always having to talk, and a crowd of people takes all the magnetism and life-enterprise out of me. I don't mind the essential teaching, tho' I abominate "lecturing," if only I could teach under a bushel, like a nice grey toad, with time for moonlight excursions in the grass. And so I have slipped along at Dana Hall and College, year after year, never really meaning to settle down into College work, but yielding sometimes to the pocket and sometimes to the heart, always intending to drop out presently into office work or country school teaching or some form of simpler, less absorbing occupation, by which I could earn my bread and butter and chocolate creams and have time left over for *living*. I don't want to shirk my share of the work of this world, but I'm haunted by a notion that one serves God best and humanity best in growing into the character (which, after all, is the only deed) whose pattern he dimly recognizes in himself, and vaguely believes God fashioned there.

Still, it was never very possible to leave Wellesley, because so many anchors held me there, and I knew that Miss Shafer [the President] tho't it dishonorable in a teacher not to return, if she could, after a year of leave. So I was fully intending and desiring to go back, if I should get strong and well, and it was with all the pain you could wish that I faced the other possibility, which seemed to darken so fast into a probability, and which Miss Hodgkins' letter seemed to make a certainty. But having let it all slip you must blame my temperament and perhaps my health that I can't make a return to Wellesley very real or joyous to myself at once, especially that people keep writing about a Professorship, for which I don't feel either intellectually ready or inherently fit. Fortunately the Trustees haven't asked me—and they will be more foolish, if they do, than their recent actions would seem to indicate—and I shall have a chance to rest and get the winter's fog out of my eyes and brain before deciding anything. There are wrong ways and right ways of going and getting almost anywhere. I really shouldn't come to you, and to all those I love, if I came for love of you to work that wasn't mine,—I should only be going away from you. That's why I'm not surer and gladder about my returning to Wellesley. But there's no discount on my joy of heart over the forward leap of the College. It is not only glorious tidings in itself, but you are happy and triumphant in it, and so are all my friends among Faculty and students, and Marion is full of contentment. It would have been such an eternal pity if that blessed girl had thrown her weight into the wrong scale—and everybody writes me that Mrs. Durant does not seem to feel outraged or distressed, as we so greatly dreaded. And almost the best of it all is that Mr. Durant's deepest purpose can now be truly attained and even a mole like myself can't easily help seeing him smile in Heaven. All the Wellesley letters I received at Antwerp, where there were two of yours, just sang for joy. And after all I suppose I shall be drifted back to Wellesley in the end, if I'm well enough. The winter has been rather retrograde, but you must not lay all that on the Wellesley anxiety,—lay it largely on those atrocious London fogs—we can hardly breathe today—and on the continual wet and cold, from which, as birds of passage, we could not always well protect ourselves,—ever since. We saw many memorable things on the Continent, but got very tired in the seeing, and I herewith renounce for the rest of my stay abroad all sight-seeing and tourist qualities. As soon as Nannie sails, which will be in about three weeks, I'm going to Oxford to rest and watch the spring. The College gardens are there and the river-banks, the boy-choirs and the Turners, the Bodleian, and lectures when I want them, too many people, perhaps, but the bulk of my American acquaintance will be gone and I shall live very quietly and do my faithful best to get well.

In a postscript to this letter a Katharine well known to her family and friends spoke briefly: "What's the American Academy of Political and Social Science and *why* on earth should I want to join it."

At the end of the trustees' deliberations there had been only two dissenting votes, Mrs. Durant's and one other. Moreover, a full professorship was voted Katharine unanimously in June. Mrs. Durant, in time, was to say of her, "I love and honor that noble Christian woman, who is the soul of truth." But no word came from her until April, and Katharine, assured by Mrs. Guild that she would hear from Mrs. Durant and also receive formal notice of promotion, had time for further reflection. She wrote her mother from Antwerp:

It looks now as you will see by the enclosed note from Marion as if I should return to Wellesley, if I am well enough. I am very tired at present, but it has been a severe winter. I never suffered so from cold before. I hope a quiet spring and summer in England will make me vigorous again, but there would be no wisdom in returning to Wellesley for another breakdown. As for my other letters from the college, they are from personal friends and all, of course, urge my return,—except Miss Julia, who thinks my literary salvation lies in a prompt withdrawal. Well! Time will show. I only want to do right. . . . I suppose for long I shall have to carry my nervous system carefully, like a cracked pitcher, but perhaps I can do that at Wellesley as well as anywhere. It seems to me a little hard on Wellesley, though. I'm afraid going back means a long goodbye to any original writing. It is *such* a busy, feverish place. But I'll do my best there, only I can't help dreading it. It's not that I don't love Wellesley. I should be very glad to go if I felt more equal to the responsibilities of the position.

The letters Katharine received from the college made it clear that Miss Hodgkins would resign and that she would be appointed her successor. The department would then consist of a group of women with differing religious convictions but with the utmost courtesy and kindliness toward one another's opinions. She knew and loved both Vida Dutton Scudder and Sophie Jewett, and she could now write with eagerness and anticipation as the spring wore on: "There is absolutely no end to what can be done in my new position at Wellesley. If I could only study a few years more before undertaking it."

Katharine's decision was entirely her own. Her mind was completely independent, and she was, as her letters make clear, uninfluenced by the fact that others strongly urged her to accept the Wellesley offer. She had within her that core of resistance which Henry Adams a few years later was to mention as an ingredient of the New England character, and, possessed of what she called her "genius for minorities," she was perhaps more strongly tempted than even her mother knew to stay in Europe indefinitely and turn away from her future at Wellesley.

A definite decision was not made until spring. Meanwhile, Katharine and Nan made the most of their weeks on the Continent. In Paris Katharine, at Nan's urging, lingered somewhat halfheartedly before the shop windows. Nan commented, "You've improved and yet there's something *lacking* in the way you look at shop windows." But she did have pleasure in buying such gifts as her resources allowed, which included a Paris doll for Arthur's little girl and gloves for Jen.

Descriptions of cathedrals again fill Katharine's journal. She "loved the devotees, but couldn't love the gilded, tawdry altars and missed the grey, naked majesty" of England's great houses of worship, "where, in turn, I had missed the very splendor and devotion that half attract and half repel me now." Everywhere the travelers went they visited cathedrals, admiring architecture and stained glass, but wearying of the relics and looking with skeptical Protestant eyes at "cabinets of little bones of saints," skulls, girdles, ropes, and chains. In general they followed Baedeker and saw the things they were advised to see.

Their brief itinerary took them through Holland and Belgium, with first a trip to Cologne. They cared most for Amsterdam, which Katharine found to be a thrifty, homey city. She took time from the Rembrandts and other Dutch paintings to visit the Zoological Gardens, where she divided her attention between the strolling Hollanders and the baby lions and cockatoos. The Hague was royal and handsome, but too luxurious and modern. A happy day was spent on the beach at Scheveningen watching the herring fleet go out and the children sailing their wooden shoes in the sandpools.

At Antwerp they attended mass at the cathedral when the Rubens paintings were uncovered. Brussels was gay despite the recent death of the young Belgian crown prince, whose picture, framed in purple pansies, could be seen everywhere. They spent hours in the museums and at the Palais des Beaux Arts, lingering in the Rubens rooms where "horror contended with splendor."

Van Eyck's great altarpiece was the supreme attraction in the cathedral at Ghent. From there they went to the Beguinage, the largest of the remaining convents of that charitable order. Here they bought lace and talked with some of the "chatty little ladies" who took them over "one of the simple little houses with its saints, crucifixes, pictures for the penitential pilgrimage, black window-curtains and black bed-curtains, and the photograph of the young prince, over whose death they were afflicted like fond aunties."

The hurried, crowded trip was good to look back on but wearing to live through, and it was with real relief that Katharine wrote of "a beautiful, blue crossing and the white cliffs of Dover," and of London, "the coziest great city in the world with almost no noise at its heart."

Nan was to leave her now, and after a few days in London the friends went to Oxford where Nan packed and reluctantly said goodby. Katharine settled down to work. She was studying by herself, attending lectures occasionally, and writing. Since she felt that a full professor should not concern herself with juvenile literature, the sequel to *Rose and Thorn* was abandoned.

Happy as she was to return to Oxford, the first joy and delight had passed. An intellectual sophistication had replaced the eager sentiment with which she had begun the fall term. The dream of Oxford which possessed the minds of young American scholars in the latter years of the nineteenth century was only partially fulfilled. The undercurrents were not deep and full, and the "trail of philology" was "over it all." English, like other modern languages and literatures, was not given any attention, and no degrees were awarded for English scholarship. The situation was deplored by her English friends, who, however, laid the blame on the literature itself, which could not be interesting if Oxford failed to make it so. Oxford itself was beyond criticism. Nevertheless, although Katharine knew that lectures and tutoring at home could very well stand comparison with what she found at Oxford, she felt that "the rich privileges of the Bodleian, the inspiring beauty of the venerable, many-towered city, and the subtle intellectual influences in the air" compensated "for any real or imagined lack in the English lecture-rooms or elsewhere," and her "heart was not large enough for receiving it all." It might not be worth while to go to Oxford for literature, but it was "a thousand times worth while to go to Oxford for Oxford."

After receiving a letter from Mrs. Durant asking her to return to Wellesley, much of Katharine's time was occupied with plans and preparation for the courses she would teach. There were also plans to make for the summer. She had proposed that Jen join her in England and return with her in late August. Gifts and the proceeds from her writing had made possible a longer stay, and a check for Jen from the aunt for whom she was named opened the way for her, too, to have a vacation. Delighted by the prospect, Katharine wrote, "My heart isn't quite pressed flat in a Middle English dictionary." She urged her mother to come too, but Cornelia was content in her daughters' letters and preferred what Katharine called the "better side" of the Atlantic.

She continued her correspondence with Miss Hodgkins in a friendly, courteous vein, but the gay, personal little notes and letters ended. Katharine was hurt, but she could not cherish a wrong or bear a grudge, and the two remained friends and correspondents for many years. Before Miss Hodgkins' death she said to a friend of Katharine's, "She has been as a dear daughter to me always." Many years later she sent Katharine's executors a handful of letters from which the answer to that "intolerable letter" was omitted. Only one, evidently written to soften the effect of the December letter, makes any reference to the matter. Katharine wrote a charming reply to this one about her travels and impressions, dropping just one sentence into the middle of a page: "If I took to myself more pain from your Christmas letter than was just to you, I am sorry." The episode was ended and she was returning to Wellesley. But she was a different Katharine. The youthful gaiety and spontaneity with which she had begun her wonderful year of travel and study had given place to a sober and more reserved mien. Gone were the days when Nan could prompt her to "run whooping like Red Indians, and in sheer joy, down an Arran hillside, surprising the browsing sheep." She had grown intellectually and spiritually in spite of an occasional feeling that the year had been "retrograde." She was ready to face the new responsibilities awaiting her when she returned home.

As usual, she sought her relief from weariness and worry in the open air, or in the services at one or another church or chapel. A typical entry in her journal is that of April 25: "Little sleep of late and bad head, all lead and feathers. Studied in a weakly noodle-headed fashion, and then walked to Iffley meadows, where I found 'snakeshead,' gowans, buttercups, and genuine, blessed dandelions. The river was haunted by white-breasted, blue-backed swallows. Went to Christ Church for vespers and was deeply comforted by the anthem: 'They that wait upon the Lord shall renew their strength.' "

To a friend she wrote of these services: "I like Magdalen best, for the altar-painting of Christ bowed beneath the cross. It is only a faint glimpse of it I can get in the many-twinkling candle-light, but it is better so, for the eye might be offended, but the heart can only worship the better in the presence of the symbol of the Christian ideal."

The last months went far too rapidly. Jen arrived with a small party of friends, so Katharine, now in excellent health, was able to continue her work at Oxford and joined the group only for the last three weeks. As the summer drew to a close, she wrote her mother: "Two weeks from this afternoon my long exile is over and I turn my face toward the blessed shores of America and toward you."

XII

"America the Beautiful"

WHEN Wellesley College was established, its statutes asserted that it "was founded for the glory of God and the service of the Lord Jesus Christ, in and by the education and culture of women." By 1890 the religious emphasis had increased. Although the original statutes required Evangelical church membership of the teachers, apparently this provision was not enforced, since in 1890 amendments to the statutes were proposed by the trustees to carry out Mr. Durant's original purpose. One amendment provided that every member of the faculty hold membership in an Evangelical church, another asked full "sympathy with Evangelical views as commonly held by Protestant churches," and a third suggested only that teachers be of a "decided Christian character and influence."

It was the last amendment which was adopted in February, 1891. Mrs. Guild's cablegram had brought the good news to Katharine. The records do not show why Mrs. Durant delayed writing to her until April, or why the executive committee did not vote her appointment as full professor until June. Miss Hodgkins' reservations about Katharine must have been well known and were doubtless given a good deal of consideration, especially by Mrs. Durant, who had preferred the stricter amendments. Although she never held the presidency, Mrs. Durant was a trustee and held the office of treasurer of the college. As one of Wellesley's founders, her opinions were deferred to by the entire college body. It is not difficult to imagine the indignation meetings held among Katharine's friends that year, the theological arguments, and the factional divisions in the student body and the faculty. The situation was no secret, for many besides Mrs. Guild were writing to Katharine.

As her letters indicate, Katharine was not entirely satisfied with her life as a college teacher. But the other half of the balance was heavily weighted, and she had the ability to accept a situation and achieve happiness in it. She was returning to New England, and that alone meant much to her. "The scenery that is most beautiful to me is the scenery to which my eyes are most wonted." The landscapes at home had a "shyer, more elusive beauty" than the grander scenery, softer colors, and warmer horizons of England. "[As] through the living faces we watch we come to know life, so at Wellesley the woods and waters become revelation. A divinity shines through them."

Upon her arrival home Katharine hurried first to Portland with her mother and Jen for a family reunion. Gifts were unwrapped, the chronicles of her journey brought up to date, the new baby in Arthur's family admired, and the Paris doll presented to "Tot," her older niece.

Then Katharine returned to her Wellesley office and classroom and to the warm greetings of friends. She wrote at once to Miss Hodgkins: "Freshmen and Freshmen and Freshmen! You have sent us all generous hints and helps, the books are in beautiful condition, but I think we all feel rather *waify* and as if we were playing school. There are inquiries on inquiries for you. When I have time to write, be sure that you will hear. Meanwhile the love of the orphan-department.

Dazedly K.L.B."

Although courses in English literature were not required at Wellesley at that time, over half the student body elected work in the subject, and the new head of the department was

Katharine Lee Bates
about 1900

America the Beautiful

O beautiful for spacious skies,
For amber waves of grain,
For purple mountain majesties
Above the fruited plain!
America! America!
God shed His grace on thee
And crown thy good with brotherhood
From sea to shining sea!

O beautiful for pilgrim feet
Whose stern, impassioned stress
A thoroughfare for freedom beat
Across the wilderness!
America! America!
God mend thine every flaw,
Confirm thy soul in self-control,
Thy liberty in law!

O beautiful for heroes proved
In liberating strife,
Who more than self their country loved
And mercy more than life!
America! America!
May God thy gold refine
Till all success be nobleness
And every gain divine!

O beautiful for patriot dream
That sees beyond the years
Thine alabaster cities gleam
Undimmed by human tears!
America! America!
God shed His grace on thee
And crown thy good with brotherhood
From sea to shining sea!

Katharine Lee Bates

happy to welcome Margaret Sherwood as a fourth member of her staff. She wrote a note to Miss Hodgkins, reporting progress: "The Department has not struck a rock yet. Our smooth sailing is due in chief degree to the beautiful order in which you left everything. The unwariest pilot couldn't easily wreck so well-mannered a ship on the first league out. Miss Jewett is a fountain of refreshment and withal the most methodical of the four. She and Miss Scudder most beautifully supplement each other as poetry versus philosophy. . . . Miss Jewett is sometimes down-hearted . . . but her discouragement proves her ideal,—height by depth. Miss Sherwood is doing fine work. Miss Bates is a 'no-count sort of Professor, and we all feel still decapitated."

The students who were attracted to the English literature department were fortunate indeed, for the four women who constituted its staff were of exceptional character and ability, and all were to become well known in American letters. Miss Scudder had come from Smith, and Miss Sherwood from Vassar. Miss Jewett, who was in large part self-educated, had gained her wide knowledge in her father's library and in the great libraries of Europe. Katharine later likened Miss Jewett's teaching to "handmade lace whose exquisite quality no Ph.D. machine product can equal." All four teachers left from time to time for further study abroad and brought honor and fame to the college through their degrees and publications. The department was soon one of Wellesley's strongest and remained in that tradition.

Katharine's time and strength went immediately to the attempt to realize the ideals she had envisioned during her last months in Europe. Her family situation partly helped and partly hindered her. Cornelia and Jeannie either kept house for her or boarded in or near Wellesley. Cornelia looked after Katharine's material comfort and welfare, nursed her in illness, and kept the "ragamuffin" mended and presentable, while Jeannie became her typist, a post she held nearly all her life. In return, Katharine's strong sense of filial duty prompted her to devote many hours to her mother and sister, which meant countless midnight sessions at her desk. For her family's sake she entertained village and college friends, learned to play whist, and took her mother for drives in the woods about Wellesley.

Her position and her published work had extended her reputation rather rapidly. Many magazines requested articles on literary subjects, on various phases of the education of women, and on life in a college for women. Her hands were so full and her days so crowded that she sometimes wondered why anyone ever read or wrote. It seemed to her that her days went to "odding and ending." "Seven days shalt thou labor," she wrote, "and not do half thy work." Her journal records that she "growled through Council," was "ugly" to her staff, quarreled with the President, and taught her classes nothing. Thoroughly ashamed of her behavior, Katharine wrote out a set of resolutions during the summer vacation which she vowed to carry out when she picked up her Wellesley life in the fall: "I must give more heed to the outward appearance, dress better, walk better, etc. I must keep a more even mood of courtesy. In the home and in the village I must be more careful of the small pleasantnesses of daily life. I must study more lovingly my mother's comfort. I must respect individuality and most of all my own. As regards the College, I must study reserve. Reserve is, or may be, strength, and strength is what people want. I must look to my own growth, as the duty of duties. I must not let myself be a drudge for conscience's sake."

But life was not all drudgery for Katharine. There were entries in her diary that mentioned days when she was "much comforted by much kindness," when the understanding of friends and colleagues and the close, congenial associations in the department made the hard work seem trivial.

College life, so absorbing and so increasingly demanding, took nearly all her time, of course. But there must be time as well for writing. The small salaries of the day made the extra labor a necessity. Maintaining a home was expensive, but it was her mother's greatest desire to live with Katharine, so the effort must be made whenever possible. Arthur helped as much as he could, but he had a family of his own, and there were other relatives who must be assisted. Therefore, Katharine met the requests for articles and continued to work on special editions of the classics. In these years she edited three of Shakespeare's comedies in the "Students Series of English Classics."

In 1893 Katharine took up the notes from her year at Oxford and began work on the pre-Shakespearean religious plays, which were published in that year under the title *The English Religious Drama.* When she was asked to lecture at the summer session of Colorado College, she organized some of this material in lecture form and in the heat of early July started on her first western journey. She stopped briefly in Chicago to visit Katharine Coman's family and spent the better part of a day at the World's Columbian Exhibition. The exhibition had become widely known as the "White City," an architectural symbol of cities that might rise as a result of man's aspiration, and the gleaming white buildings made a lasting impression on Katharine. After this brief visit she continued her journey. On July 4 she wrote in her diary: "Fertile prairies. Hot run across western Kansas. A better American for such a Fourth."

When Katharine arrived at Colorado Springs, she found herself among a congenial group, which included Hamlin Garland, William J. Rolfe, and Woodrow Wilson in whom years later she was to see the "Champion of Peace" and the symbol of hope for all nations. She began her teaching "under the purple range of the Rockies," surrounded by scenery of indescribable beauty and with the "White City" fresh in memory. Some three weeks later these impressions flowed together to become her best-known poem.

"America the Beautiful" is the inevitable expression of Katharine's idealistic love for her country. Though the poem was inspired by special circumstances, the feeling that shaped it had long been a part of her, ready to be transmuted to poetry when the exact moment should arrive. The story of the writing of the hymn has been told many times—how Katharine joined a party to make an expedition to the summit of Pikes Peak in a prairie wagon. She has written of the incident: "Our sojourn on the peak remains in memory hardly more than one ecstatic gaze. It was then and there, as I was looking out over the sea-like expanse of fertile country spreading away so far under those ample skies, that the opening lines of the hymn floated into my mind." Before she left Colorado the poem, together with the rest of the summer's output which she described as "disheartening," was completed and shut away in her notebook.

Another poem written during the western trip, "Year of the Vision," was directly inspired by the "White City." Here, too, she was moved by a longing for an idealism that would pervade the life of her country, by a vision of "alabaster cities" symbolic of that idealism, and by a faith that men who could build that "circle" of "glistening domes" would lead America on to "sweeter life and purer passion." The final stanza,

Oh, sting our souls with this diviner need
And, ere thou fadest, take our high decision
To make thy radiant dream immortal deed,
Year of the Vision.

is infused with her deep desire to turn dreams into deeds and to find in every deed the dream. This is the ever-recurring theme of her poetry.

Katharine's patriotism was characterized by an idealistic conception of her country. Poems written before "America the Beautiful" express this sentiment, but in no arresting way. Some of the earlier poetry remained in scrapbooks; one or two she preserved in collected volumes. A long poem, "Land of Hope," catalogues some of the natural beauties that she loved: "Mountains, rock-based, cloudy-crested . . . prairies aripple with wheat." America as "the Beautiful" had not yet appeared; the exact moment had not arrived. But the vision was there, to be seen in sudden flashes of intense feeling which might possess her as she walked the streets of a foreign city or gained the first glimpse of her native shore when she returned from an alien land. Not Spain, her second country, nor England, her second home, could hold her beyond a few months' stay. She was always eager to return to the land which she believed would one day become a "pure, august, authentic commonweal," a "Pioneer of Brotherhood among the nations." She was never absent from her country in spirit.

"America the Beautiful" was put aside for two years. In 1895 Katharine sent it to *The Congregationalist*, where it appeared on July 4 and attracted immediate attention. For some time Katharine considered the criticisms and suggestions which came to her from all over the country and finally rewrote some sections. The new version was then published in the *Boston Evening Transcript* on November 19, 1904. Later the opening quatrain of the third stanza was altered, and the poem in that form has remained the official version. In her rewriting Katharine could not alter, in response to criticism, the word "beautiful." To her America was, quite simply, beautiful, and as always she used the word that exactly expressed her thought. She retained the copyright to protect the poem from misprints and "conscious alterations," but she never accepted a fee for use of the hymn after the original payment by *The Congregationalist*.

As the years passed, letters to newspapers and to the poet poured out afresh, inspired by the contest held by the National Federation of Music Clubs to select a musical setting for the poem, and by the movement to adopt it as the national anthem. Opinions varied from that of the reader who called the poem the noblest expression of patriotism ever uttered by an American to that of the gentleman who found the poem maudlin and preferred instead a hymn embodying the spirit of "*aux armes, citoyens!*" Word by word it was taken apart and criticized. Katharine should not rhyme "proved" with "loved," the word "beautiful" was hackneyed, and the lines

God mend thine every flaw,
Confirm thy soul in self-control,
Thy liberty in law!

might show a "praiseworthy sentiment," but they were "entirely lacking in the divine afflatus." The phrase "crown thy good with brotherhood" contained a "hint of letting down." Katharine remained aloof from the controversy but replied as best she could to the flood of letters and, amused by the extravagance of the request, even wrote the poem in longhand ten times for a correspondent who asked for copies for each of his ten grandchildren.

The poem's hold upon the affections of the public grew steadily. World War I gave great impetus to its progress, and with the advent of radio its popularity was assured. In 1926 the past presidents' assembly of the National Federation of Music Clubs launched their contest to obtain a musical setting for the hymn. Katharine refrained from any expression of opinion, though she approved of the contest. Nearly 900 compositions were submitted to the judges, but none was found worthy of selection. The contest did not exclude original compositions already well known in certain sections of the country. That of Will C. MacFarlane, municipal organist of Portland,

Maine, found the greatest favor and was widely used. The setting by Clarence C. Hamilton of Wellesley's music department has been sung at the college for many years, and it is probable that Katharine secretly preferred it because of Mr. Hamilton's association with Wellesley and her long friendship with him. However, she made no public statement of preference. Today the poem is most commonly sung to the music of "Materna," by Samuel A. Ward.

While the contest was in progress, the National Federation of Music Clubs and the National Hymn Society pressed in separate actions for its adoption as the national anthem. Many strongly-worded letters were written both for and against the proposal. The long use by the general public and the armed services of "The Star Spangled Banner" made it inevitable that Congress should eventually choose the older song and establish it officially. But no country is necessarily limited to one national anthem, and it soon became evident that public affection for "America the Beautiful" had given it an unofficial second place. Its extensive use in schools and churches, its adoption as the official song of the National Federation of Women's Clubs, and its popularity in the two wars have established it firmly as one of our best-loved and best-known songs.

There have been many requests for information about the poet and the circumstances under which "America the Beautiful" was written. Despite Katharine's efforts and those of others since her death, garbled versions and fantastic stories still are current. Such tales reached the height of absurdity when a radio sports commentator described Katharine as a famous woman athlete who entered a walking contest on Pikes Peak and was so exhilarated when she reached the summit and found herself the winner that she promptly composed the entire hymn. This piece of nonsense would have amused the author, who would object far less to such misrepresentation than to the plagiarism that is occasionally attempted, sometimes naïvely, more often deliberately.

The great popularity of the song, Katharine believed, was "clearly due to the fact that Americans are at heart idealists, with a fundamental faith in human brotherhood." And that remains the best explanation, if one is needed. It is often said of the poem that it expresses for the millions of Americans their loftiest ideal of patriotism. For them, it rejoices in the gifts of their great country, it honors their dead, it pays homage to their past, it utters their aspirations, and it lifts their prayers. It is truly an American anthem.

For all her idealism Katharine was not unaware of reality. In "Year of the Vision" she saw more in Chicago than the "White City." She knew that beyond it lay a "troubled gloom" where its "dark neighbor" felt the breath of a "bitter wind." In her poem "America the Dream," in the volume of that name, she affirms her faith in her country and realizes that centuries must pass before her ideal can approach reality. "Oh, to redeem from our America's still folded eyes the marvel of her undiscovered dream!" The eyes of love are not blindfolded, she says, "Their vision clear discerns more flaws than keenest hate has known."

Much has been said and written of "America the Beautiful" in the years since 1895. Perhaps the best summation of its worth was written by Katharine's old friend and fellow townsman, Gamaliel Bradford, in an editorial published in the *Boston Herald* not long after Katharine's death: "There is [in the poem] the deepest, richest sense of the splendor of the material possession that has been given to us, and the impress upon every American citizen, every man, woman and child, to be worthy of that possession, to sustain it, to consecrate it, to ennoble it by developing the great qualities that can alone make any nation beautiful in the eyes of those who understand what spiritual beauty is."

XIII

England Again

The English Religious Drama established Katharine's reputation as a scholar. Until its publication she was known primarily as a writer of magazine verse and stories for young people, and in the schools she had gained some reputation as an editor of the classics. This volume, a condensed discussion of the evolution of the early plays, gave her added fame and was very well received by the critics. Katharine was particularly commended for the manner in which she clarified the indebtedness of Shakespeare and his contemporaries to the earlier dramatists. The book was recommended to the student of Shakespeare, who could profit by a brief discussion of Latin liturgical drama and the miracle and morality plays. Katharine's style was generally praised, and she was complimented for her achievement in making a normally dull subject picturesque and interesting. In the section on the morality plays Katharine frankly advised that they should be read "with a bookmark at the last page. When the jaded brain, for nothing tires like stupidity, is capable of no other delight, there is still a shamefaced pleasure in counting the leaves that intervene before that blessed goal." But in regard to the miracles, she could not agree with James Russell Lowell, who found them "dull beyond what is permitted even by the most hardened charity." While Lowell felt them lacking in drama, Katharine saw them as "nobly dramatic in range and spirit" and created an aura of drama about them through her lively reconstruction of the manner of their presentation. Although her scholarly critics failed to find new research in the book, they were well pleased with the general arrangement and competent handling of the material. Katharine received many warmly appreciative letters from colleagues in various universities and felt well repaid for her labors in the Bodleian, where, resisting the constant temptations of the summer weather outside, she had spent her "irrevocable mornings of poring over tedious pages."

Katharine's life at Wellesley did not always flow smoothly. From time to time there were strong inducements to leave. Among her masculine friends were some who entertained "matrimonial sentiments," and occasionally she received proposals of work elsewhere. One of these came from the Macmillan Company, offering her the editorship of a projected literary magazine. She finally declined this position, perhaps because she had come to feel that her future lay in teaching, or perhaps because she feared that she would have even less time to devote to writing than her present position allowed her.

On one occasion during these years, Katharine did resign from the college. The reason for her action is not known, but in any event, Mrs. Irvine, president of the college at the time, told her she was "bound to stay" and persuaded her to remain for one more year. Henceforth Katharine evidently ceased to contemplate a move. Yet she often described herself as a "reluctant captive" with a "wayward fancy." She was evidently seriously disturbed and had great difficulty in holding herself firmly to what she felt must be her destined course. At length, however, she put her doubts behind her and wrote with determination:

If one of us two must break,
The luck that seeded my sky

England Again

With stars malign, or this heart of mine,
I swear it shan't be I.

This troubled period was happily broken by a summer at Oxford. She released her "tugging little balloons" in June, 1894, and sailed to England with her close friend Katharine Coman.

Although the work of this vacation was to be primarily devoted to her edition of *The Merchant of Venice,* she was turning her attention as well to a book which she later considered her most scholarly achievement. She had been asked to edit two plays by Thomas Heywood, *A Woman Kilde with Kindnesse* and *The Faire Maid of the West,* for the drama section of the "Belles Lettres Series," which was under the general editorship of George Pierce Baker. Owing to the exigencies of her teaching and to the necessity for prolonged research in England, work on this edition was extended over a number of years. "Old Heywood," as Katharine called him, became almost a member of the family. The voluminous files that began to accumulate were kept in a large mahogany cabinet known as "Heywood's House," and the family followed his career with interest.

However, her summer's program was too full to allow any real beginning on this project. The major part of her time was to be taken up with *The Merchant of Venice* and a book on the early secular drama, which would be a companion volume to *The English Religious Drama.* There were two lectures to prepare and two articles to finish. She intended to read some Goldoni every day and a few pages of German, and somehow or other she must find time for long walks. As for her verses, she must "find poems growing on the hills." Eventually the book on secular drama was abandoned in favor of a projected work on American literature. Despite her good intentions, the editing of *The Merchant of Venice* was the only large task completed that summer. But she was well satisfied with this accomplishment and called it "a very fair edition." Others went beyond this modest estimate and spoke with genuine admiration of her conscientious scholarship.

When they arrived, England was damp and murky—Oxford, situated in the river valley, exceptionally so. Both Katharines were affected by the prolonged wet weather and were finally forced to leave the Walton Street lodgings to go to Headington, a short distance away. Here, on a sunny hillside, they found a pleasant four-room suite. While her friend convalesced, Katharine walked back and forth each day from the "Bodley" and brought the mail which had arrived from home and news of their circle of acquaintances.

Katharine also had her share of physical ills during the summer, including some rather painful sessions in the dentist's chair. She wrote her mother, in what she called a "disgustful digression," a graphic description of her experiences:

This old goose of an Oxford dentist assured me that the nerve was not exposed and filled the tooth, which in a few days began to jump like mad. I went to him again and, in much bewilderment, he knocked out "the stopping"—not a pleasant process with an infuriated tooth—and helplessly put in a quieting dressing. This afternoon I went again, and a young assistant appeared, saying that the dentist felt "a little hill, 'm" and had sent him to change the dressing. This youth poked about in an inquiring and agitating manner and found the exposure. He said the tooth had been filled right on top of an inflamed nerve and now there was nothing to do but kill the nerve. I don't think either of them knows Boston baked beans about dentistry, but it's the best place in Oxford, and they say the American dentists in London are perpetrating horrible charges. I can't afford to put my whole letter of credit up a tooth. I've wanted to see Dr. Allen [her dentist at home] more than any—*man* in America. If I ever cross the ocean again without being overhauled by my own dentist on the wharf! Well! I let this callow executioner put in a dressing to kill the nerve. He says it will produce acute inflammation and for an hour and a half I shall suffer "violent hagony." So I turned back from the Bodleian and came meekly home for my suffering, but the "hagony" doesn't report itself yet, altho' the tooth keeps up a grumbling threat. I have to go to them tomorrow, when they expect to remove the nerve, but they shan't do it unless the nerve is happily defunct. They are of the "lower class" and stand in convenient awe of their patrons,—not so Dr. Allen. But in this chair I retain command and, when they hurt, tell them that is all they "can do at present." They "must apply a palliative," and they hastily acquiesce. But I would rather have an intelligent despot.

The friends were troubled by the news from home. The Chicago Pullman strike was in progress, reported in lurid detail in the English newspapers. Miss Coman's brother was in Chicago, and while "her sympathies are, as always, with labor against capital, she doesn't want her brother murdered or his business destroyed." For a time their talk was all of Governor Altgeld and President Cleveland and his use of federal troops. While Katharine listened sympathetically to her friend she privately felt that there were two sides to every question and that after all there was something to be said for capitalism. Occasionally she accompanied Miss Coman to London to attend socialist meetings, and once she heard Karl Marx's daughter, Mrs. Aveling, expound her theories from a perch on a rickety chair in Battersea Park. But time was passing rapidly, and finally she refused to attend such demonstrations.

Several of Katharine's close friends were socialists or very sympathetic to socialist theory, but she herself was always a conservative who limited herself to a deprecation of certain class distinctions—an attitude which might be described as a matter of taste and courtesy rather than a political position. An illustration of this attitude appears in a letter to her mother:

I am sitting on a stump, out on the open meadows, just outside the village of Wytham, some three or four miles from Oxford. Katharine and I started forth after our frugal lunch of gooseberry tart and cheese, with buns and cheese-sandwich "biscuits," writing materials and poetry books, an opera glass and a local guidebook, all in the old blue shoulder-bag. First we walked along the Thames to Godstowe, where the nunnery stood in which Fair Rosamond ended her erring days. There are only a few ivied walls left now and these serve as an enclosure for cattle. Then we took a raised path between hawthorn hedges, frequently broken by inconveniently high stiles, and jumped off a fence into the "model village" of Wytham. The lord of the manor, Lord Abingdon, lives in the "Abbey," which means that when Henry VIII dissolved the monasteries, he gave one of their beautiful estates to this noble family. Visitors are sternly excluded from even a sight of the dwelling and extensive parks, —all being walled about to the height of some ten feet. But we were more interested in the village, where some two hundred souls live in pretty thatched cottages, over-grown with roses, and worship in bare pews in the little church, while the gentles occupy the great, cushioned "manor pew," behind which is the rector's pew, also graciously furnished with a cushion.

These remarks are typical of her occasional mild social criticisms. In the plain pews of her father's church in Falmouth there had been no cushioned seats for gentry, and her concept of the brotherhood of man was rooted in her early days in the friendly little village, where the inhabitants "practised a neighborly socialism without having heard the term."

With the arrival of American papers the travelers' fears about the state of their country were somewhat allayed. The

English papers had reported Chicago looted and in flames, but Katharine had a "very different feeling reading the reports in papers that contain, side by side with the account of disorders, the ordinary news of a civilized country." They talked of events at home with American friends who were constantly coming and going in Oxford:

We have been having rather a blue discussion this evening, and have come to the enlightened conclusion that rioting must be put down, that immigration must be stayed, that the labour party must be directly represented at Washington and that our best men must go into politics and purify them. We have not, however, cabled this to President Cleveland, of whose assassination I daily dread to hear. We hope these London papers exaggerate, but there must be some basis for their frightful stories.

In a letter to her brother Sam she wrote:

We have discussed American politics and English politics over our breakfast jam almost every morning this summer and come to the conclusion that England's advantage lies in the fact that her best men are proud to go into politics as a life-profession. A man like John Morley, distinguished in literature, or James Bryce, with the stuff of a great historian in him, drops everything for the direct service of his country. Both men are in the ministry at the present time, one as secretary for Ireland, one as president of the local board of trade, and every day, from three o'clock in the afternoon till midnight, sees them hard at work in the House of Commons. The House of Lords, to be sure, is hated hard, and next Sunday there will be a monster meeting to denounce it in Hyde Park, delegates coming from the chief cities of Ireland and Scotland as well as from England and Wales. It is supposed that four hundred anarchists have entered England from the continent during this past week. I understand that we are preparing to shut them out of the United States. That is all fair enough.

No house can be asked to receive as guest the man who come to burn it down, but I can't help feeling sorry for a young man, like Santo, whom Society kills for killing and hates for hating. It really isn't educational to chop off a boy's head—for the boy. It is a confession of weakness, a clumsy way of disposing of a difficulty. If Society was wise and strong and good, it would be able to convert its criminals into men instead of into corpses.

I hope these sentiments will not lead to my being refused the privilege of landing in Boston. I don't want to assassinate even Mr. Pullman. And I am glad to observe that I am prouder of your molten image, Mr. Cleveland, than I ever expected to be.

A new occupation provided comic relief for a summer of work and worry. Miss Coman hired a bicycle and Katharine a tricycle, and the two friends went for five-mile rides about the countryside in the long Oxford evenings. Miss Coman was thrilled with her new accomplishment. From her safer perch Miss Bates surveyed her friend's bumps and bruises with concern but agreed that they should both take to bicycles in the fall. Miss Coman, determined to go the whole way, returned from London one day with a pattern for "bicycling trousers," and Katharine sent her mother some of the newspaper correspondence which was inspired by the appearance of women upon the roads in this adaptation of male attire:

In the London Morning Chronicle, A.D.B. of Oxford declared fiercely that if women wanted the truth on this subject, he would give it to them. The figure of a man is beautiful, but a woman's "legs and front of her back" are grotesque and ugly and, if a woman has any sense of decency, she will only be too thankful to hide herself in skirts. "Artist" retorts that sculptors have copied woman's form in all ages, and A.B. returns the crushing reply that it is much easier to sign yourself "Artist" than to be one, and sculptors have made mistaken experiments in all ages. "A Mere Male" suggests that A.B. give God a few points on the making a woman, whereupon A.B. responds that he has made no mention of God in the matter and considers such allusion sacrilegious, to which "A Mere Male" replies by begging his pardon for supposing that "A.B." thought God made women, whose author, judging from "A.B.'s" opinion of the sex, "A.B." most likely holds to be the Devil. Meanwhile "Women Cyclists" of all ages and opinions have been giving their experience of torn skirts and broken limbs, or of tailor-made skirts that never catch on anything and refuse to blow in any wind. "A Man" has expressed his hope that Parliament will forbid the rational costume, whereupon the "New Woman" has flung herself upon him in a body, declaring that Parliament can't, won't and shan't, and if it does all women will wear knickers in revolt against the "tyranny of man." In vain the "Countess Hugo" has taken the pen to inform women cyclists that their appearance is SHOCKING, in vain "A Young Bachelor" has asked why it isn't a matter for the fathers and husbands and brothers of the individual women to decide, and equally in vain "Truth" has assured poor womankind that men are not only better in physique and brain, and always have been, and always will be, but they possess the inestimable advantage of being in the minority, the supply being less than the demand,—that a woman's one chance of happiness lies in marriage and that her one chance of marriage lies in being "as feminine as possible" and dressing prettily, as men like to see her dressed,—that many women cannot marry, anyway, because there are not men enough to go around, and that if any woman says she doesn't want to marry, it is disgraceful and she ought to be ashamed of herself. So the correspondence which has been running for a fortnight, a dozen earnest, indignant and savagely sarcastic letters appearing every morning snarled itself up in a war of the sexes and was terminated yesterday by the editor.

Miss Coman might concern herself with costume, but Katharine, seated modestly in her tricycle, wore her skirts comfortably and devoted herself to reducing by means of this new exercise, for, as she sadly informed her brother Sam, she was overweight, "notwithstanding my five mile spins, but when I have taken two thousand, I may lose half a pound. You know our father used to say that it is 'the manifest destiny of the Bateses to be fat' and, judging from Uncle William, we can't look to the Lees for deliverance. But one day we shall be nothing but souls and then I expect to be, as Mother predicts of Jeannie, 'a very slim angel.' "

The few summer weeks were over far too soon. But the edition of *The Merchant of Venice* was completed and Katharine had achieved a rest from routine. She left for home with renewed love for "cozy, uncomfortable England" and a "great respect for the race that, reaching out from this soggy little island, has conquered and civilized so much of the earth and has produced the United States." With this "modest climax," and a last word to her mother, "I mean to be a better child to you the next thirty-five years than the last," she closed her last letter and embarked upon the homeward voyage. It was a fair crossing and she sat in her steamer chair and outlined her plans for the fall: "The Shakespeare class must work, but we must also comprehend. I must bind the hours in a closer unity. In the Chaucer class I must lay more stress on beauty, less on fun, and we *must* have exact information." Her schedule filled all her time and left only Sunday afternoon for extras.

The long days at sea gave her the last rest of the summer. A few hours in the salt air always brought her renewed strength. She spent much time on the decks, watching the "level plain of restless blue." Fittingly enough, one day in the far-distant future a Liberty ship, the "Katharine Lee Bates," would ply these waters she loved so well.

XIV

"A Loving Despotism"

KATHARINE now presided over a department organized according to her own plan, which had been carefully formulated over a period of years. Many of her ideas about educational processes stemmed from her first year at Oxford, where teaching methods varied widely from techniques at home and gave her her first opportunity to consider the larger aspects of education in general. She had written to a friend at the time urging that faculty members come to know and understand one another. "The faculty will be more strengthened by union, which shall develop and call into action the power that already is." As for college teaching she said, "I don't believe in education much, only when it works by evolution, not by dogmatism. Freedom and strength will not prevail until we recognize the candor and clarity of the thought-process as of more moral value than any formulated conclusion." She wished that note-taking, and even books, could be excluded from the classroom, for "There is something in the living voice that books, to the majority, do not give." Above all, the student's mind must open ever wider. "The mind sins that suffers itself to think timidly and obscurely."

Miss Scudder has described Katharine's achievements in the English department:

A firm and admirable foundation had been laid by Louise Manning Hodgkins, but hers had been the day of small things, and now growth was swift. . . . Always the problem was faced as it will be faced by education to the end of time, of uniting flexibility and freedom for the student with some sort of rational co-ordination in her study. It is an arduous problem. How Katharine Bates worked at it! I see her through those first years, gracious, vital, strenuous, inexorable in her demands on herself and on others, rejoicing in the adventurous sense of the pioneer. There was nothing static about her; always she was moving with the times. . . .

While decisions were hers to make, and were made firmly, so far as the general shaping of policies was concerned, she left to the individual teacher absolute freedom for the untrammelled play of creative power so far as his or her course was concerned. Her mind was essentially a very conservative one; her clinging reverence for established ways sprang from her fine power of discerning their best values. But if mind and temperament were conservative, they were also hospitable, and she had a delicate regard for the convictions and methods of other people even when they failed to commend themselves to her; except when she felt that some higher good was imperilled. Her despotism was a loving one and always courteous. She attached people to her personally, even when she wasn't giving them what they wanted.

The quest for minute accuracy was pursued with unflagging zeal. But conscientious as she was in these ways, she never for a moment lost or allowed us to lose the sense of great imaginative literature as something dynamic and potent. She did not present her students with a problem to solve but with an experience to enter, which is a far more exacting and strenuous matter, and demands a higher discipline. And the distinctive quality about the department of English Literature at Wellesley under her administration, a quality that gave it perhaps a special status all over our country, was just here, in the infusion of scholarship with the very spirit of life. Miss Bates was a great humanist.

It has been noted that in the early years of Katharine's chairmanship students were not required to study English literature. Therefore, it was inevitable that as each college year began she and her associates received a clear indication of the measure of their success in the increasing numbers of students who enrolled in the department. For those who chose to specialize in the field, an orderly schedule of courses was outlined: "A course in Anglo-Saxon for the Freshman year, followed in turn by the Chaucer course, the Shakespeare course, and a course either in Georgian and Victorian poetry or in Victorian prose, with a concluding course in the development of English literature." The program was supplemented in alternate years by one-hour lecture courses in American literature and poetics. In addition, there were advanced seminars conducted by the Chairman, Miss Sherwood, and Miss Scudder.

Of the last two, Jeannette Marks, a former student and later a professor at Mount Holyoke College, has written: "To do advanced work with Margaret Sherwood was to discover depth under depth the meaning of what it is to be a student and to love learning somewhat as the ancient Greeks must have loved it. . . . An inspired personality . . . is Professor Vida Dutton Scudder, the liberal thinker, a devout Christian, an eloquent teacher, a shining essayist."

From time to time Katharine was called upon to describe the department in articles touching upon the life of the college. The aim of the department was, in her words, "to secure on the part of its students an appreciation of the best that has been thought and said in the world of English letters." In this aim the four teachers were closely united. They became widely known as an extraordinary group of women. Martha Hale Shackford, a student in this period who later became their colleague and eventually chairman of the department, wrote of them:

Of very varied individualities, they had in common, wide acquaintance with literature and life in America and Europe, and unusual gifts of swift penetrating insight into significances, accompanied by the power of sensitive yet challenging expression. . . . In the classroom, the Academic Council, in the Literature Office, or in social groups, they were notable for flashing wit, keen analysis, perfect urbanity, interest in national and international affairs, and unfailing sympathy with a just cause, or with misfortune of any kind. Incomparable teachers, accomplished scholars, authors of books, poems, essays, with more than local reputation, they have given to Wellesley that which Time can never take away.

The only textbooks used by the department were the masterpieces under consideration. There were, of course, outlines and bibliographies prepared by the teachers, plot diagrams, comparative tables, systems of prosody, and literary maps; but these were considered merely the working tools of well-directed study. Beyond the comprehension of content lay "the mystery of passion, the apocalypse of imagination," which could not be taught, nor even, when most deeply felt, discussed fluently, yet which must be subtly conveyed. As the student stood upon the threshold of full awareness, Katharine advised, quoting an Egyptian proverb, "When thou makest a voyage to the stars, go thou blindfolded; and carry not a sword, but the sandals of thy youth."

"The student who proposes to specialize in English literature" she wrote, "should make her beginnings at home and in the nursery. Let her learn by heart, poetry and prose, the best, and all she will. Keep the Sunday papers from her and the nickel magazines, but feed her young imagination with the myths of Olympus and myths of Valhalla, Hans Christian Andersen, old ballads, Homer, *The Faerie Queen,* the *Pilgrim's Progress,* the *Arabian Nights,* the *Alhambra.* Let her know Roland, Sigurd, Cid, Don Quixote. . . . Read Scott with her and Shakespeare. . . . Save her, in those sensitive years, from the cheap, the flimsy, the corrupt in books. Every hour spent in reading trash is not merely so much time wasted, it is so much fineness blunted, so much dignity of mind debased. . . . We live the earth life but once, and in important matters it is intolerable that we should be put off with the second-rate. . . . But there must be two parties to a bargain. Literature is a generous dealer, yet it exacts a price. We must lift at least our wonder and desire to the level of a Ruskin, a Carlyle, before the wind of their great inspiration can envelop us and beat us free of pettiness and falsehood."

The problem of liberal teaching, she held, was "to make knowledge play into life, to serve as nutriment for growth and independent energy." The teacher's part must be twofold. The students were to be held to "the strait path of exact knowledge."

Of Katharine's teaching Miss Shackford wrote:

> We who were undergraduates during the years when she established the major in English literature were constantly impressed by the range of her reading, the remarkable tenacity of her memory, the scope and aptness of her allusions, and, most of all, by her sensitiveness to aspects of imaginative beauty. Yet her awareness of ideal values did not prevent her from being a teacher who gently but firmly demanded from students sound knowledge, scrupulous accuracy of detail, and fastidiousness in form. Though often seeming shy in the classroom she was, when roused by argument, unmatched in repartee. Always there was a certain piquancy, in her conduct of a class, due to unexpected, stimulating modes of approaching a subject, and she was capable of gay and teasing innuendoes regarding the stolidity of some of our appreciation of great literature.

Katharine took great pains with her teaching and administrative duties, but the seminar was the greatest pleasure of each week, for here she could offer the garnered wisdom of all her years of study, research, and experience to those who would best understand and appreciate it. In this atmosphere of intimacy students were awakened to creative effort and in return gave back to her all her bounty. She did much more than spread before them the treasures of literature; she gave them, too, her ideals of kindliness, generosity, courage, and love. One of her students wrote of the meetings, "Those hours were as choice a distillation of the spirit as this fleeting, burden-filled world will ever offer."

The seminar, which was held in Katharine's home, often lasted, as one of her students shamefacedly confessed, four or even five hours instead of the allotted three, so engrossed and stimulated were both students and professor. Study was devoted to the great Elizabethan and Jacobean dramatists and was always varied, for Katharine disliked a stereotyped program. Katharine's friend and neighbor Gamaliel Bradford often joined the group and remained an occasional member until Katharine retired in 1925. At the final meeting Mr. Bradford presented a sonnet to Katharine, written as a tribute to many a rich discussion and spirited battle of wits:

English Drama Seminar 1924–1925

A many-colored winter, full of things,
Things tragic, things poetic, things dramatic;
A touch of melody which soars ecstatic,
Transfiguring the wide world while it sings,
A touch of medicine which bites and stings,
A shower of questions, more or less Socratic,
And always drama, English, Spanish, Attic,
Have made the hours float by on silver wings.
But what has winged them most is her quick wit

And gracious wisdom governing our course,
Till wayward petulant fancy ceased to flit
And carping question lost its cunning force.
Only sometimes I wish that she would stretch her
Large charity to cover poor John Fletcher.

The background for the busy life of the college was the pleasant home on Abbott Street, which was shared for some years with another '80, Charlotte Fitch Roberts, Wellesley's gifted and outstanding professor of chemistry, and with Miss Coman, who often joined Katharine in the long walks that were so essential to her well-being of mind and body. "Lucifer," her bicycle, carried her flying to and from the college every day, and to these two forms of exercise she added golf for a time, which she found "the best fun out," recording confusedly in her diary, "Played six links today."

Of all the formative influences in Katharine's life, the out-of-doors had been primary. In childhood she had watched, only half aware, the progress of each year from season to season. As cares and responsibilities pressed upon her in adulthood, she consciously sought distraction and solace in the natural world. The colors, sounds, and movements of nature delighted her senses and refreshed her spirit, as in the woods or on the hills her eyes looked deeper and followed the long vistas and misted horizons until she caught

Those swift illuminations when we see
The flying shadows on the fragrant meadows
As God beholds them from eternity.

But such poetic expressions were rare during these years, for Katharine could spare very little time for poetry. She was much in demand as a lecturer for literary groups in near-by towns, and what free time she had was devoted to research and writing. *The Merchant of Venice* was followed by editions of *A Midsummer Night's Dream* and *As You Like It.* These works were received very favorably by the critics, who found her scholarly discussion greatly enhanced by her charming and enthusiastic style.

With Lydia Boker Godfrey, of the Wellesley library staff, she also published *English Drama: A Working Basis,* a bibliography of the secular dramas. George P. Baker of Harvard wrote her that he regularly referred his students to this work, and offered for her use the notes he had made in his copy in the event of a new edition. Bliss Perry had "great pleasure in its thoroughness and convenience for reference" and called it "an admirable handbook for the student."

In 1897 Katharine's lectures on American literature were published in book form. The completion of this volume was Katharine's last major task before she left for Europe on sabbatical leave. *American Literature* was written primarily as a textbook but was also issued without the classroom appendix as a volume for general reading. The book covered the literary products of the Colonial and Revolutionary periods and the National Era and closed with a discussion of realism in the novels of Henry James and William Dean Howells. The appendix was a valuable contribution to the field and was generally approved by the reviewers. Many critics thought the work was the best on the subject to that date, fair-minded, well proportioned, and written in a vivacious and spirited manner. It was considered an eminently readable reference and was welcomed with special satisfaction by schools and colleges.

The Nation took a different view from that of the majority of critics. While conceding that Katharine "was not often in bad taste," they accused her of "blunders of the first magnitude" and concluded their adverse remarks with the statement that she showed evidences of possessing a literary skill worthy of a better book.

English reviewers found the "reading of her book decidedly pleasant," although they considered somewhat amusing her assumption that American literature was truly "American."

Katharine sailed for Europe at the close of the college year in 1898. She was traveling alone for the first time, but she had friends who would meet her abroad. As usual, she had many plans for work and research on the journey. She never allowed herself to be an idle traveler, for, as she wrote,

I was loath from all that Pleasaunce of the Sun,
and its words and ways,
To come to my country giftless, and showing no
fruit of my days.

She now had a considerable body of scholarly work to her credit, much of it the result of her trips abroad. She had never returned "giftless" and would never so return.

XV

Spain

KATHARINE'S educational interests were not limited to Wellesley College. She was a director of the International Institute for Girls in Spain as well, and this circumstance was in part responsible for her decision to spend several months of her leave in that country, though the school had moved to temporary quarters at Biarritz because of the Spanish-American War. The institute was founded by the Reverend and Mrs. William Hooker Gulick, an outgrowth of their missionary work in Spain. Mrs. Gulick had become deeply interested in the education of Spanish women and had opened the small nonsectarian school at Santander. It was later moved to San Sebastian, and, after the stay at Biarritz, established permanently at Madrid. Mrs. Gulick was a graduate of Mount Holyoke, and many of the women who became active participants in the growth of the school were friends of Katharine's at Mount Holyoke and Wellesley. A league was formed in the women's colleges to arouse interest and secure the support of "enlightened womanhood." Katharine was one of the original directors of this organization and gave generously of her time and energies to the undertaking.

In preparation for the journey she had begun Spanish lessons during the winter and had persuaded her mother to join her. Mrs. Bates continued to study the language for many years and later gave her daughter much assistance in correspondence and literary work.

The first six months of the sabbatical year were divided between London, where Katharine lived at 11 Torrington Square, a square of poetic association since the days when Christina Rossetti lived there, and Paris, where she found a comfortable pension at 6, Rue de la Sorbonne. Research in the libraries and museums and Spanish lessons occupied most of her time. For rest and refreshment during her stay in London, she went occasionally to Malvern and to Oxford. There was never an opportunity for loneliness or homesickness, for American friends were constantly coming and going in London, and English friends entertained her. She was studying the records of old sea voyages in preparation for a collection of ballads about the early adventurers. This project was often put aside for more important work and was never completed. Though she did little sight-seeing, she did vary her schedule with long walks and bus rides about London, and she went regularly to services of the Church of England.

The London visit was saddened by the death of Katharine's friend Mary Sheldon Barnes, who had been a history teacher at Wellesley when Katharine Bates was an undergraduate. Mr. and Mrs. Barnes were working in London that summer, engaged in research and writing, and Katharine often visited them. Mrs. Barnes's sudden illness and death brought a sense of great loss to Katharine. The familiar mystery of life she lived gladly, but the mystery of death she was never able to accept with complete resignation. In her younger years she could not agree that "there is no name, with whatever emphasis of passionate love repeated, of which the echo is not faint at last." The early loss of friends and classmates, gifted women whose lives were full of promise, hurt her unbearably, but in her grief she drew closer to other friends, aware that "God is never kinder than when He gives us burdens too heavy for us to bear alone." The words were Katharine Coman's, and Katharine wrote to her in reply: "This world cannot spare its idealists, its precious personalities. I feel the walls of the world contract. The street sounds are coarser and harsher than ever. There are so few people who care chiefly for ideas and live purely in hope and love."

Katharine's journey to Spain was not without some hazard because of the war, but Mrs. Gulick and others felt certain that she would be unmolested, so she went on with her plans and crossed to France early in October.

She studied four languages at the Berlitz School in Paris, French, German, Italian, and Spanish. To obtain practice in Spanish conversation, she went to the Convent of the Assumption where she "met a pleasant, sensible English 'sister,' who arranged for my Spanish lessons, at three francs an hour. Then she brought me in the dearest little sister from Manila, wan and big-eyed, speaking no English and almost no French, but chattering Spanish like a hundred squirrels in one. I could understand hardly a third of all her eager prattle, and it nearly broke my heart not to understand, because she was telling the story of Manila. But I'll get it again one of these days, when I know more Spanish.

"Poor Spain! The papers say tonight that el Señor Rios consents to the Treaty of Peace. But my little Nun doesn't! She told me in very emphatic Spanish that she was indignant, indignant, indignant. All these years the Spaniards had been working in the Philippines, Christianizing the heathen, and then we came with a terrible big fleet and took their islands away. I did not try to explain our new imperialism in Spanish. It troubles me not a little to understand it in English.

"I went to her again today and carried her a white rose, for tomorrow is the feast of All Saints, and we have given these poor Spanish cause to mourn many dead. I suppose she could not keep the rose, but would like to lay it before one of the shrines. She was cold in that chilly room, the little Castilian who had been five years in the Philippines, and she looked very weary, but when I asked if she were cold, if she were tired, she only clasped her little hands and said, 'But these things matter not.' Whenever I go to her we chatter away in Spanish in friendliest fashion, although she looks upon the United States as a nest of bandits. She is a lovely little sister, brown-eyed and brown-faced, worn from her late experiences of war and travel, but with the old religious ardors and ecstasies in her eyes. They are always shining, however weary the face in its soft white folds may be. She has never seen her parents since she entered the convent. She will never see her childhood's home again. 'These things matter not. The world passes. In Madrid, in Manila, in Hong Kong, in Paris, it is all one life to us who have entered the secret of the everlasting peace.' "

Mr. Gulick, who had business in Paris, came to see Katharine to discuss her Spanish trip. Spain was in the forefront of the American mind at the time, and the *New York Times* was to print a series of letters from Katharine if the editors found them worth-while. Since the letters would make a travel book on a timely topic, she was very eager to fulfill the assignment. The United States diplomatic service in Spain was, of course, interrupted, but the Gulicks and their many Spanish friends would provide perhaps ever better sources for the necessary information and experience. She wrote her mother: "Mr. Gulick has been spending the evening with me. In view of the continued sittings of the Peace Commission, I had put off my Spanish trip indefinitely. He tells me I am very wise to wait but that the way will probably be opened in by January. He has been here to urge the claims of the Caroline Islands on the Peace Commission."

Katharine sought what Spanish contacts were to be found in Paris, partly to add to her knowledge of the country and its people, and partly to keep herself occupied. She had learned that for an American "the European solitude breaks us all down, more or less and sooner or later." She always learned much about a people in their churches; therefore, she attended Spanish Catholic services whenever possible. "Sunday afternoon I spent two hours in Queen Isabella's Spanish chapel. The place was thronged and the worshippers exceedingly devout. There were beautiful Spanish women there and elegant Spanish dress. I'm going there Wednesday morning at eight to the commemorative services for the dead. I shouldn't think they would mind an American prayer in a corner, would you?"

Great actors and great plays drew her to the theater wherever she might be, and in London and Paris she was able to see the finest of the men and women who enhanced the brilliance of the stage at the end of the century: Sir Henry Irving, Ellen Terry, Coquelin, Modjeska, Mme Réjane, and Sarah Bernhardt. But still the dutiful daughter, she wrote her mother on the eve of her fortieth birthday: "My professional Sabbath-breaking has not yet begun, and I shall keep the theatre out of the Sunday, if I can. I am going to the Comédie Française Tuesday evening to see Molière's L'Avare, and have half-decided that I would better take the late hours and double bills rather than confuse our Puritan traditions with Sunday matinées. But I'm waiting to hear from you before finally deciding. To my own conscience, seeing a great play, as a work of art,—all art being essentially worship,—is not a bad way of keeping Sunday, but it's the old question of other peoples' consciences and feelings. Consciences are queer. I have been to church twice today, this morning to the American Episcopal Church. I enjoyed the service, but the sermon was a weak little appeal for more money to make the church prettier. And when I went to Vespers at the Catholic Church of the Madeleine this afternoon,—a magnificent church with a splendid ritual and music,—a man thumped me in the midst of my devotions and demanded three cents for my 'pray-God chair.' It's awfully hard to keep Sunday in Paris."

The most single-minded student in Paris could not but be aware of politics. To Katharine this aspect of European affairs and conditions was full of interest. And, of course, anything touching Spain and her own country was of first importance. "Midnight, but no peace in this fevered city. The streets are deep with mud, for it has been raining, raining, raining nobody remembers how many days, but all Paris is out howling, 'Viva Zola! Viva Picquart!' and the opposite. The Senate is to sit all night and the streets about it are one turbulent mass of roaring humanity. The naughty Parisian newspapers are beside themselves with mirth over Félix Faure and his acceptance of the Spanish queen's honor of the Golden Fleece. Now, they say, he has 'joined the Spanish sheep.' "

In answering to her mother's question she wrote: "No, I do not exchange lessons with the Little Sister. She doesn't want to know anything I know! My new hat is brown and soft and feathery. I don't keep my stockings *much* mended, nor *many* buttons on, but I get along. My laundry is done once in ten days by a woman Madame employs. She keeps it ten days before returning the greater portion. There's always something that doesn't come back. Madame says it's something I shouldn't have put in."

Her mother received, too, accounts of her educational experiences: "This afternoon I went to the Sorbonne for Gebhardt's lecture on the Spanish drama. Very French performance. Famous man. Crowded room. Much wit, waving of hands, turning of petty phrases and the like, but nothing new on this subject. I tried another man on Spanish Drama at the Collège de France. He really had a list of books to give, but nobody seemed to take notes, and the bell rang before he had finished, and nobody seemed to care—except himself. He said he regretted it very much, but we all hurried out. I recognized the academic atmosphere."

The Christmas season came, and Katharine took time from packing to write home of the Paris holiday: "It has not been a bad Christmas at all, at all, although I am so far away. I had picked up trifles for the family at the pension. It's always great fun shopping in France. People are so gay and crisp and verbally polite. They may hustle you and they may cheat you, but their tones are so brisk and dapper and their turns of phrase so pretty. Madame was out of humor, which made dinner difficult, but in the evening Monsieur took me to the midnight mass at the beautiful church of St. Sulpice. I had to pay six cents for my 'prayer-chair,' but as I occupied it from nine o'clock till one, the amount per hour was not excessive. It was a very impressive service, with beautiful music. I found flowers in my room and a stocking in the chimney piece and when Madame came in to kiss me in the morning because it was Christmas, I said, pointing to the fireplace, 'But see what Santa Claus has brought me down the chimney!' and she answered: 'Has he? What a nice little Jesus!' We had an English Christmas dinner and later I went to the Convent and attended their Vesper Service,—the sisters, with wax candles in their hands, and their long veils of white shading into the cream-white vests and violet robes, swaying and bowing in the music like lilies in the wind. After a chat with my own little sister, who is sure all Protestants go to hell, I came back to the heart of the city, where the Rue de Rivoli was gay with shops and lively with shoppers."

After the holiday season Katharine was off for the sunshine and surf at Biarritz, where she heard all the news about the school and conditions in Spain and mapped out an itinerary which would take her from one friendly home to another in city after city.

The fortunes of the International Institute were intensely interesting to Katharine. Mrs. Gulick's purpose from the beginning had been to overcome the terrible illiteracy of the middle and lower classes, and her efforts had met with an impressive measure of success. Her work was sustained by a nonsectarian corporation consisting of American educators and other interested citizens. She returned to the United States from time to time to speak on the needs of the school and to recruit assistants. Katharine had long known and admired her, and it was with the keenest pleasure that she now watched the school in operation and met or renewed acquaintance with the teachers and administrators. She took a small part in the educational program, addressing a seminar in fluent Spanish. Early in February she said her goodbyes and crossed the border to San Sebastian.

On this journey Katharine saw religious persecution for the first time. The plight of the Spanish Protestant shocked and dismayed her. Among her French Catholic friends she had met only kindness and courtesy. Not so in Spain. Here she heard Protestant Christianity attacked from the pulpit by priests "who know what they do, and why they do it." She listened to a "Franciscan friar, a fervent preacher and a man of high ascetic look, thunder out in the face of a vast congregation, that 'nowhere, though one searches the world over, can there be found a work of mercy,—hospital, asylum, refuge, endowed school, university, charity of any sort or kind—established by Protestants.'" Such effrontery in public statements was hard to bear. Equally dismaying were her personal encounters with cultivated Spaniards who were amazed by her statement that Protestants actually prayed, and who asked if it were not true that they "denied Christ and spat upon the Virgin."

A new Protestantism was taking root among the people. It did not spring from the Protestantism of old, which had been literally done to death by the Inquisition. The Spanish Protestant whom Katharine came to know suffered for his religion. His chapels were defaced, his schoolroom windows broken;

he was denied work and refused promotion; he paid higher rent and was treated with scorn. But Katharine's faith in education and the power of love led her to believe that such ignorance and prejudice could be overcome.

Drawn to this land and its people by her own warm-heartedness, she adjusted herself quickly, and sincerely attempting to understand the religious position, she went her way as traveler and observer. She was almost invariably taken for an Englishwoman, which saved her discomfort and embarrassment; but when she was recognized as an American, she found that Spanish courtesy was extended even to the enemy. She was not a missionary and had no zeal to convert. "Know your own bone," said Thoreau, and to this saying she adhered. But, since her vocation was to set forth the truth, she suffered acutely in the face of Spanish bigotry and illiteracy, shocked to note "the popular identification of Protestantism with all that is impious and criminal."

The evidences of backwardness in education troubled her deeply, and she was equally distressed by the gross deficiencies of the press and the falsification of war news. In a letter to her mother from Granada she quoted a news despatch of a day in February:

> The North Americans carried the day, coming out ahead by reason of their superior numbers and equipment, but with an immense loss in killed and wounded. When they had finally repelled the attack of the noble sons of liberty, the Yankee oppressors avenged themselves for their losses, like cowards, by assassinating anywhere and everywhere in the streets of Manila all the defenceless natives whom they met, and especially the women and children, among whom they made a horrible slaughter. General *Ottis* vainly hurries forth fresh proclamations to allay the terror caused in the North American troops by the heroic valor of the Tagalos. The panic prevailing in Washington is tremendous.

She went on to describe her explorations:

I have wandered about these wonderful old ruins, and passed through peasants' tumble-down kitchens into beautiful old walled gardens with Moorish fountains. I have even explored the cemetery, from which I met the grave-digger returning with the empty coffin on his shoulder. Not only are the poor buried without coffins, but often the gypsies strip them of every shred of clothing. I chat with the peasant women as they cook their *puchero* —their earthen pot of cabbage and peas and whatever else comes handy—over an out-door fire, and I argue with the beggars on the error of their ways, and I watch the small children at their games, and exchange the courtesies of the day with the "Gypsy Prince," who flits about the hill in gay attire. I often roam through the enchanted halls of the Alhambra, and I climb about the strange old staircases and winding ways, and sometimes come out by chance into a garden where the south wall is overgrown to twice the height of a house with red roses and great branches laden with yellow oranges. It seems so strange to see blowing over these old, old stones, tumbled and lichened and broken, the young, young petals of the new peach-blossoms. There are few trees about,—olives in abundance, with their "little gray leaves," and the elms that Wellington planted here, and poplars, a tree which Spanish legend says is the Adam of all the trees, the first that God created. The thrushes sing in the garden under our windows and very soon the nightingales will come.

Katharine soon grew to love Spain and its people. The letters published in the *New York Times* described the country, the people, and their customs, and served in place of detailed letters to her family as well. The few letters to her family were brief and personal. They betray hints of boredom brought on by the anxiety at home that she might be molested, that she might unwittingly eat horse meat, or that she might become a Roman Catholic. But she patiently reassured her mother, reminding her that she was forty years old and could remember to put on her rubbers. She minimized the discomforts, the attacks of grippe, the "fleas as big as cannon balls," the appalling dirt. She surmounted them all, and took Spain and its ways to her heart, meeting everywhere Spaniards who were hospitable, generous, and kindly in their efforts to explain their country. When, as occasionally happened, she found herself in an uncomfortable situation, she murmured to herself the old Spanish saying, "Feet, why do I love you?" and went rapidly on her way. She was frequently escorted by Spanish gentlemen, friends of the Gulicks', who found her unmarried state deplorable. She was told that if she did not marry but kept all her wisdom shut up within her "shining brows," she would be like "God in His loneliness before He created Him a Son."

In July she was joined by Katharine Coman at Biarritz. But Miss Coman was not well and could not stand the modes of travel and the accommodations to which Katharine was now accustomed. It was soon clear that the last weeks of the Spanish journey must be given up, a keen disappointment to her since the well-planned letters would be cut short. It meant, too, a serious loss of income. But her friend's welfare was of first importance, so assuming the role of anxious nurse, Katharine moved Miss Coman to Vigo. She had hoped that the sea air would prove beneficial, but conditions there were not suitable for an invalid, so the friends boarded an English ship in Vigo harbor and returned to England, Katharine overwhelmed by the unfamiliar cleanliness of her surroundings. Two weeks at Malvern restored Miss Coman, and Katharine finished the last letters for which she had notes. They sailed for Quebec at the end of August, and Katharine had time for a visit to Portland before she returned to Wellesley.

XVI

Joy and Sorrow

WITH the coming of September, Katharine was immediately "immersed in the academic," in the departmental meetings, Council, classes, and "all the weary rest of what isn't poetry." October was perfect in "color and brightness, but I had to keep my ecstatic nose to the academic grindstone." She was, nevertheless, "glad of the college" and settled down near Miss Coman in a tower room on the campus. Her mother and sister were in Portland. What energy she could spare from college duties was devoted to the preparation of the book on Spain, and she was also beginning work on a fourteen-volume edition of Hawthorne's romances, which entailed a separate introduction for each volume. Articles and lectures on Spain were much in demand. It was always hard for her to refuse a request that she share any special knowledge, experience, or gift she might possess, and she responded generously. When Mrs. Gulick returned to the United States, Katharine felt that she must help her in every possible way—which meant many committee meetings and speaking engagements away from Wellesley. In addition she was continuing her Spanish lessons so that she might be even more proficient in the language on future trips abroad.

Spanish Highways and Byways was published in 1900. Based on the letters she had written for the *New York Times*, the book was reviewed with appreciation and commendation.

She had called it a "record of impressions," but to her readers it held even more of value. Published so soon after the close of the war, when Americans felt a special interest in Spain, it enjoyed a gratifying success. The critics found in it an understanding of the people and the life of the nation as a whole, and prophesied for it a lasting popularity. The strength of the work lay in the author's keen perception and sympathy, and in her talent for bringing the country and its customs before the reader in felicitous and captivating prose.

Partly to amuse herself she began writing poems under the pseudonym James Lincoln, taking the surname from an ancestral line, the Lincolns of Hingham. "Jay" had a post-office box in Boston, and she decided that his career showed promise when Bliss Perry accepted a short story for the *Atlantic*. "Jay" wrote both prose and poetry and was successful for several years, finding a later welcome to the *Atlantic* when Ellery Sedgwick published a sonnet. Katharine eventually acknowledged her authorship when she included some of "Jay's" poems in collections.

She found diversion in the homes of village friends. The Bradfords and Mr. and Mrs. William C. Norcross welcomed her often. As time went on their babies were, perhaps, the chief attractions of their households. Mr. Norcross had been a friend of high-school days, and Mrs. Norcross a classmate at Wellesley. Katharine often visited the Misses Eastman, and there were gay evenings with the Rotherys, whose family life Agnes Rothery described in *Family Album*. And in the home of Mr. and Mrs. William Ladd Taylor she listened to music and watched the progress of Mr. Taylor's paintings, for which Wellesley residents served as models.

The college year 1899–1900 had begun with the inauguration of a new president, Caroline Hazard. Of course, Katharine attended the ceremony in the new chapel, but she "tired of it all presently and slipped off" to her room, never suspecting that a new friend had stepped across the threshold of her life. Miss Hazard was one of the most loving, generous, and thoughtful of all Katharine's friends. Possessing the means as well as the heart for a generosity that was not only deeply sincere but wisely practical, she observed many ways in which she could ease the problems of living for Katharine. On her own birthday she made it a custom to drop on her friends' desks what Katharine called a "golden feather." She had no experience in the difficulties of making both ends meet, but sensitiveness to these matters in a friend's life was discerning and unobtrusive. With infinite grace she made her practical gestures of friendship and regard.

For a year Katharine Coman, assuming a "responsible dean-look," held the office of dean of the college, a position later held by Ellen Fitz Pendleton, who was to succeed Miss Hazard. Miss Pendleton ("Nellie Pen" to Katharine), who had graduated from Wellesley in 1886, was a mathematics teacher, but her ability in the administrative field was recognized early in her career. After her year as dean, Miss Coman became head of the Department of Economics. Through these friendships Katharine came to know intimately many phases of the college life outside her own field.

For the most part, these were contented years, for Katharine was essentially a happy person, and she had already realized success in her writing and in her teaching. Added to the buoyance of spirit with which she was able to greet each new day was a love of fun, a childlike quality which was never smothered by the responsibilities or dignities of passing years. She spent as much time as she could with children and never missed an opportunity for play. She was always ready, in the mood of one of her poems for children, to "toss my satchel across the gate." She escaped from the day's drudgery into whimsicality and delighted in every kindred spirit who would abet her in fun and nonsense. Quite conscious of the therapeutic value of her ability to turn back the clock, she invented nicknames for her friends and names for her rooms, set up her intimate household gods, and created her own diverting symbols, courting the "simplicities of mirth" and finding in "the childish ways of love" relief from her exacting duties. She loved to give parties, especially for children, to write valentines, to send gay little verses with the books she returned to the library. She never escaped by shutting her door, as another New England poet did, saying "It's just a turn—and freedom!" She welcomed solitude, but primarily for the opportunity it gave for poetry, and since solitude was rare in her life, she learned to write her poems on the daily rounds, on trains, or at odd moments during the day. They came, as she often said, "by accident."

But in spite of a natural aptitude for happiness, Katharine became increasingly conscious of the tragedy of life. At first this awareness had come to her in personal sorrows. Then study and travel had made her acutely sensitive to the "whole of distress." She acquired an "apprehension of a universal ignorance and inadequacy." Insomnia and her susceptibility to minor debilitating illnesses played some part in this facet of her temperament, which she constantly strove to keep from her friends. Her large sympathies attracted many troubled people to her, and she listened patiently to their tales of sorrow, lying sleepless for hours after her visitors left, her mind filled with the scenes of suffering they had described, seeking solutions to the problems they had brought to her. It continued to fall to her to write memorials and tributes to deceased members of the college body, and she often finished last tasks in connection with books upon which friends had been working at the time of illness or death. Very often a mood of melancholy enveloped her at such times.

However, Katharine had at her command a determined spirit in the face of undermining influences. As years passed she consciously developed various ways of dealing with any tendency to depression. It was not her instinct to submerge sorrow. She met it squarely and put it into words without self-consciousness. Poetry was her natural mode of expression, and into it she poured her grief, her uncertainties, and her longings. It was for her a catharsis of the spirit, and many of the poems written to ease the flooding emotions were so personal that she never allowed their publication. Her threnodies and requiems were poems of anguish, of groping, of the search for faith. They were as natural an utterance to her as are the manifestations of sympathy of less articulate persons. Through her suffering and her aspiration of mind and spirit her character was enlarged and ennobled. A narrow grief she sought to put from her, for to give way to it, she felt, was to cease to serve God. "Gladness," she said, "hath always favour before God, and is acceptable unto Him." Miss Scudder once said of her, "The most abiding word that seems to belong to her is Courage." She had Barrie's "lovely virtue" in good measure. One of the last poems she wrote was on Courage, the quality which she called "the Saint that walks with me."

Meanwhile, she grew more and more into awareness of the companionship of those who know loss and grief, who love poetry, or whose experiences and interests draw them together. She liked the remark of a fellow-poet who said that a poem or a book is a call across country to one's kin. This sense of oneness became ever stronger in her, and she wrote:

Feast me no feasts that for the few are spread,
With holy cup of brotherhood ungraced.

More and more as the years passed she shared her life with others. The prejudices of race, creed, or color were truly meaningless to her. Those who crossed the threshold of her door were shorn of all such distinctions. Her interest lay in the individual. Her assumption of the essential goodness in every human being resulted in an unconscious striving to become one's best self in her presence. As she listened to the talk about her fireside or on her tree-shaded porch, she had a way of leaning forward with a graciousness of manner, giving quiet, courteous attention, and seeming to draw out one's best conversation.

Thus did Katharine cultivate gladness and transmute sorrow into growth. She did not shrink from life's hard experiences, but absorbed them, and through joy and grief sought wider understanding and deeper awareness of spirit. She wrote one of her best-loved poems on this theme:

For Deeper Life

Dear God, our Father, at Thy knee confessing
Our sins and follies, close in Thine embrace,
Children forgiven, happy in Thy blessing,
Deepen our spirits to receive Thy grace.

Not for more beauty would our eyes entreat Thee,
Flooded with beauty, beauty everywhere;
Only with keener vision that may greet Thee
In all Thy vestures of the earth and air.

The stars and rainbows are Thy wondrous wearing,
Sunlight and shadow moving on the hills;
Holy the meadow where Thy feet are faring,
Holy the brooklet that Thy laughter fills.

Not for more love our craving hearts implore Thee,
But for more power to love until they glow
Like hearths of comfort, eager to restore Thee
Hidden in human wretchedness and woe.

Joy and Sorrow

In souls most sullen Thou art softly dreaming
Of saints and heroes wrought from Thy divine,
Pity and patience still the lost redeeming,
Deepen our spirits for a love like Thine.

XVII

A Taste of Luxury

WITH a new century and a new president, Wellesley's second twenty-five years began auspiciously. There were changes, some inaugurated by Miss Hazard, some brought about by the temper of the times, some caused by the infusion of ideas and methods introduced by new college personnel. For the most part Mr. Durant had turned to Mount Holyoke, Oberlin, and the University of Michigan for Wellesley's officers and teachers. Many of these had left the scene during the first quarter-century, and the college now was open to wider geographical and academic influences.

Katharine became steadily happier and more at home in the growing college. After fifteen years she was so thoroughly a part of Wellesley that the earlier restlessness dropped away and the life she had chosen became well rounded and satisfying. She and Katharine Coman rented a house, which Miss Coman later bought, and set up housekeeping, sharing their home with other friends from time to time. Mrs. Bates and Jeannie lived part of each year in Portland and at other times stayed at a hotel in Wellesley Hills. Katharine took great pleasure in sharing her life and interests with her mother, and for many years they continued to study Spanish together. Jeannie, who was unable to continue her teaching because of increasing deafness, did all her sister's typing and also that of some of their friends to compensate in part for the lost income. Katharine often visited her brothers' families, and she returned once or twice a year to Falmouth.

The pattern of Katharine's life was established in teaching, writing, and travel. The edition of Hawthorne's romances was published and was followed by several other editions of the classics, together with a little volume Katharine and Miss Coman prepared for classroom use, *English History Told by English Poets.* Critics greeted this "novel anthology" from Wellesley College, "that growingly gay and festive institution for the education of women," with uniform praise.

Katharine spent most of her European summers in England, where she devoted her time to research and study. Sometimes she traveled alone, sometimes with Miss Coman, and occasionally with her first traveling companion, Miss Scoville. In her search for material for editions of two plays by Thomas Heywood, Katharine traveled tirelessly about England to parish churches, and to private libraries where the antiquarians in charge gave her enthusiastic assistance. The collections at Welbeck Abbey, seat of the Dukes of Portland, were especially rewarding. The beautiful rooms, the paintings, the wealth of historical relics, the bundles of unpublished letters, the manuscripts, quartos, and folios tempted her from her task, and she longed to linger there after the Heywood research was completed. Some of the rectors and librarians who assisted her became her friends, corresponded with her, and welcomed her on future visits. In London she generally stayed at the lodgings in Torrington Square. The Heywood research was also carried on at Somerset House. Her journal records many a "perfect day in Somerset House cellars." From time to time she was joined by cousins and friends who went about London with her to concerts and the theater.

In 1902 Katharine made a sentimental pilgrimage to the ancestral counties and towns with a cousin from the Middle West. Katharine's imagination had often played about her intrepid forebears who had made the long and perilous voyage to America, and she found the keenest pleasure in visiting the early home of her ancestors, where a saying was current that the world was divided into Europe, Asia, Africa, America, and Romney Marsh. She was disappointed to find no pirates among her "pious parents," but her cousin did discover a jurate. Katharine's knowledge of early Cape Cod history had made the pioneer days familiar to her, and the visit to Lydd, where "the great south fields of England lie smooth, as if a great palm had passed over them," revived old memories and fancies. During this journey she wrote a poem which is of interest and charm to every American:

Lydd

Far away on the sunny levels
Where Kent lies drowsing beside the sea,
Where over the foxglove as over the foam
The grey gull sails, is our ancient home.
Wide though we wander, something follows,
The cradle-call from a village hid
Under the cloud of rooks and swallows
That love its thatches and orchards, Lydd.

Here they sported in rustic revels,
Our sturdy forbears, while ale flowed free,
Richard and Susan and Sybil and John,
All their jollity hushed and gone;
Our grandsires proud of their scraps of Latin,
Our grandams, "notable huswifs" all;
We may touch the very settles they sat in,
But they, like their shadows upon the wall,

Have slipped from their sweet, accustomed places,
Stephen, Samuel, Ellen, Anne.

Katharine Lee Bates with Hamlet

The "Scarab"

A Taste of Luxury

The pewter flagons they valued so
Stand, though battered, in shining row,
But the hands that scoured them long since folded,
Lips that smacked over them, long since dust,
Are known no more in the town they molded
To civic honor and neighbor trust.

Ah, for their quaint, forgotten graces,
Flushing raptures of maid and man,
James and Alice, Thomas and Joan,
Blood of our blood and bone of our bone!
Only the trampled slabs and brasses
That floor the aisles of the old church tell
Their dates and virtues to him who passes,
How long they labored in Lydd, how well.

Their Catholic sins have all been shriven,
And their Puritan righteousness pardoned, too.
Lax and merry, or holy and harsh,
They have flown to Heaven from Romney Marsh,
Lydia, David, Joshua, Zealous,
"Katharine Spinster," yet still on earth
Their wraiths abide in our being, jealous
For the brief, blunt name and its modest worth.

For each of us is phantom-driven,
A haunted house where a glimmering crew
Of dear and queer ancestral ghosts
Quarrel and match their family boasts,
Color our hair and fashion our noses,
Shape the deed and govern the mood;
In every rose are a thousand roses;
Every man is a multitude.

Dream and Deed

A patchwork we are of antique vagaries;
Primitive passions trouble our pulse.
"Margery, relict of Andrew Bate,"
Clement, Rachel and William hate
And adore in us. No vain sunriser
In all our clan, but he owes the praise
To some progenital dew-surpriser
Who knelt to the dawn in pagan days.

Sailors that steered for the misty Canaries,
Fishers whose feet loved the feel of the dulse,
Agnes, Simon, Julian, George,
Faithful in kitchen, hayfield and forge,
Give us our dreams, our sea-love, the voices
That speak in our conscience, rebuke and forbid.
Hark! In our festal laughter rejoices
A quavering note from the graves of Lydd.

Katharine's sabbatical leave in the years 1906–1907 was filled with many new experiences. She spent the summer of 1906 with Katharine Coman in England, traveling from the Scottish border south to Land's End. The *Chautauquan* had asked for a series of articles for a home-study course on English topics, to be based on a literary journey through several famous English counties. The result was a book, *From Gretna Green to Land's End*, which was as well received as the earlier book on Spain, although one reviewer found it "hurried" and the title "uncommunicative," while another was very sorry for the "burden of learning" the author carried with her. Other critics were pleased because she copied only one epitaph and was able to keep her quotations to the point, details of criticism which amused her. Enriched by her background of earlier travel, Katharine wove the past and present together and provided a delightful experience for stay-at-homes. For the traveler she had produced a useful and original guidebook. Miss Coman advised Katharine on industrial phases of the journey and assisted her in balancing other aspects of the trip. This was one of her most successful books in popular appeal and was financially profitable.

At the end of the summer, after a few weeks in London, Oxford, and Paris, Katharine joined Miss Hazard at Lausanne for the only luxurious trip she was ever to experience. Miss Hazard traveled with a nurse-companion and always engaged the most comfortable accommodations. A long, pleasant stay in Switzerland gave Katharine the opportunity to make progress on the *Chautauquan* articles and to indulge in language lessons, cribbage, champagne, and leisurely walks. She described a day at Vevey to her mother:

We are settled down here—there could hardlier be a lovelier place—for October. I am well and busy and glad to be alive—especially in "the Vaud." This is the order of the day. At half past seven the chambermaid brings hot water. At half past eight a shiny-faced youth appears with the "little breakfast,"—a white-napkined tray with coffee, beautiful little flakes of butter, a tiny dish of honey and three rolls. I eat two rolls, put by half a one to feed to the swans when I go out, and crumb the other half over the windowledge for the sparrows. The sea-gulls swoop up and scream at me, but so far I have not seen them actually take the bread from the ledge. They are small sea-gulls, *muettes*, natives and constant residents of the lake. At nine Miss O'Brien comes smiling in with messages from Miss Hazard, whom I do not usually see till the second breakfast, at half past twelve, as I work in my room on the English articles thro' the forenoon. *Déjeuner* is a matter of half a dozen courses in the large dining-room. We sit at little tables, party by party, so that people meet very little. After breakfast Miss Hazard takes a rest, and I take a walk and an hour of French conversation at the Berlitz School. By that time Miss Hazard is ready for an excursion of some sort, and off we go exploring. Dinner is at half past seven and is quite an awful function, for which my gayest duds are by no means gay enough. We have about a dozen courses of strangely-disguised viands,—the pigeon pie, for instance, served in a pastry drum, with the Swiss flag flying from the lid; the chocolate cream appearing in the shape of a flat fish with all his fins and other individualities artistically wrought in chocolate and colored sugars; your ice cream descending formidably on you as a "Maria Louisa Bomb." It is fatal to lay down your fork for an instant during a course. The vigilant waiter behind your chair makes a pounce and sweeps away your plate. When we are finally delivered from this ordeal, there is music or something going on in the corridors. Since it is Sunday night tonight there is a juggling exhibition on hand. I went to a sacred concert in the old church of St. Martin this afternoon, but Miss Hazard was not quite up to it. So now you know how to think of me.

Miss Hazard's brother-in-law and sister, Mr. and Mrs. Nathaniel T. Bacon, arrived with their family in Switzerland for the winter and after a stay at Vevey settled at Les Avants. Their son, Leonard, one of the several young poets who became warmly attached to Katharine, has charmingly described the beginning of their long friendship:

When I first met her, I was a college freshman rusticated to Switzerland by a slight but chronic disease of the lungs. It still seems to me a strangely pleasant thing that she should have taken so much trouble about an ailing hobbledehoy completely absorbed in his own frustrations and vague ambitions. We met at Vevey in the autumn of the year. The plane trees were yellow along the lakefront, and the vineyards brown on the foot-hills. Byron and Shelley had known those mountains and sailed those waters.

Gibbon had looked out over the same slopes when the great history was finished, regretful that the gigantic task was done. If there ever was a place for enchanted conversation there it was. And she provided it. I shall not forget lightly long delightful talks about everything under the sun, about La Nouvelle Héloïse, or the interpretation of a line of Shakespeare or legends about the thousand-year-old castles that crowned the vine-smothered hills. And always my opinion invited, almost sought after, anyhow elicited quite as if it mattered. I remember thinking: "This lady is thirty years older than I, and what a good time we are having!" I'm afraid, however, I took her far too much for granted, not yet realizing how kind were the fates that had permitted me such a friendship. But at any rate I was wise enough to be excited by her permanent and catholic enthusiasms and to follow, however haltingly, strange gypsy paths she hinted at, that led without exception to remarkable and satisfactory places. There was a blank for me when winter came to shut me in amid the over-estimated Alpine snows, and she departed to Egypt. But that blank was compensated for when I found her later in England fresh from the vast experience of the Nile and openly glorying in her delicious and perennial capacity to run a little mad over a new interest, this time tomb-paintings of the 18th Dynasty.

And if she was delightful then, so she was at all times during the unclouded friendship of twenty-two years. The same vigorous and graceful humor was in her first conversation and in that last letter which by a trick of fate reached me six months after her death. There was and is no end to the knowledge, the wisdom and the gentleness, to the suggestion that opened a window on what I was too blind to see, to the admonishment with a quirk in it, that left me laughing at my own vanity. By the word spoken or written I had the advantage of that wisdom for twenty-two years, and though I may not have made the most of it, certainly I have the right to count myself privileged.

The stay at Vevey was prolonged into December, when the travelers made a hurried trip through Milan, Florence, and Rome, taking time to visit only the most famous churches and paintings. They sailed for Egypt from Naples, "landed in a general Arab row, and came through Old Testament country to a city of the Arabian Nights."

XVIII

Egypt

KATHARINE was both physically and mentally prepared for the unusual and arduous sight-seeing experiences of the coming journey. She had rested and exercised at Vevey and had spent many hours undisturbed on her balcony overlooking the lake, happily anticipating the years ahead in the house that was being built for her in Wellesley under Arthur's general supervision. She was at last to have her own home where her mother and Jen and Miss Coman could all be with her. Meantime, she had the companionship of an understanding friend who left her to the solitude she craved, and who shared the wonders and fascination of travel in new lands. Katharine recorded impressions of these months together in a series of quatrains, a verse form which had always interested her and which she advised all young poets to practice. Two of those she wrote at Vevey reveal something of her feeling for her surroundings:

Muettes

Ah, free muettes! Was it the dazzling play,
The myriad sparkle of your wild white wings,
That woke the longing for the far-away,
Alluring us to wider wanderings?

Dream and Deed

From Rôchers de Naye

Far up the forest, past the pilgrim host
Of climbing pines, tree toiling after tree,
Above the clouds we stood as on the coast
Of some primeval, frore, stupendous sea.

Upon their arrival in Egypt the little party settled down at Luxor. Miss Hazard and Katharine were both well known in certain overlapping circles, and soon to the sight-seeing was added a pleasant social round of luncheons, teas, and dinners with old and new friends, among them American scholars, consular officials, and famous Egyptologists who took pleasure in enhancing the travelers' understanding of the country and its ancient past. Miss Hazard was frequently ill with recurring Nilotic fever, but her companions escaped lightly from the disease. Katharine made short excursions from Luxor and brought back to the invalid the novel or moving experiences of the crowded hours. She was often moved to poetic expression:

Luxor

Amen and Mut and Khonsu, faintly flushed
On wall and pillar, in vain patience hark;
Their beautiful brown colonnades are hushed
Save for soft pipings of the crested lark.

She despaired of remembering even a small part of it all, but her letters captured some of her most vivid impressions:

I can't tell you what a strange, eternal look the great Sphinx has, gazing forever away to the East, with the breast worn into gaunt ribs and the mighty face battered and broken, there in the drift and blowing of the desert sands. . . . I shall have to give up trying to tell about the Pyramids—how sharply their outlines cut the sky even from far silvery distances and how they seem as much a part of the natural landscape as the low horizon hills. ... I gave one of the bead-necklaces-and-spurious-antiquities boys, who squat over against the boat-landings, a shilling to let fly a lovely little green bird, with golden-brown wings, a honey-sucker, which he told me he had caught for his supper. And the wise little bird soared up into the blue and then flew straight to the shrine of Ammon to give thanks. . . . You must come to Egypt. There isn't any way yet of doing it without large expense. My proportion, or my contribution toward the costs of the trip, is only a drop in the bucket. But I think it could be done on $250. or $300. a month. You must come. It's like nothing else under the sun. It's a land that cries out with the strange voice of a ghost and yet the voice of our own inmost life—the land of that dust out of which the human clay was made. Only from the Orient could have risen the tale that God fashioned man from the dust of the earth, but here all the land is eloquent of it. The clay huts and the slowly moving figures seem like growths out of the soil, and the Nile is the great Mother and Goddess of it all. But above this earth—"Dust thou art, and unto dust shalt thou return"—arches a glorious vast of sky, burning blue by day, and by night a golden Scripture of stars. No wonder the old Egyptians were astronomers. I dare say they are still.

Of their trip on the Nile she wrote: "There is nothing in the way of travel I have ever done so delightful as this voyaging on the Nile." The life of the river was picturesque and varied, and every stop was memorable. But Philae was perhaps the most vividly remembered of all the many experiences of the river tour:

For the first time on the voyage the river was "Nile-green": the water grew wider and deeper as we neared the dam. At a good distance from the Arabian bank of grey rocks and grey houses, lightened here and there by the white tower of a mosque, ran a long line of palms that marked the original shore. Sometimes there was only a tuft of fronds, and sometimes the fronds lay actually on the water, dying of too much abundance. Presently the rocks on the banks grew black and took on the fantastic forms of Assuan. Every now and then islands of these polished, sable, strangely-sculptured boulders peered up out of the water. And there at last was Philae, the solemn beauty of its pylons, the graceful columns of the kiosk, the colonnades submerged to their capitals, perhaps the loveliest and, at one time, the most sacred of Egyptian temples sacrificed to modern engineering. Of course the dam means life and prosperity to thousands, but it is destroying Philae. The former time that we visited it, we looked down from the flat roof, where we lunched, on beautiful reliefs and decorations gleaming pathetically up at us from under the water, and our rowers shoved us from shrine to shrine with oars set ruthlessly against exquisitely cut cartouches and the reproachful faces of Pharaohs and of gods. The drowned temple, environed by the savage banks and isles of black rocks wildly and precariously heaped,—rocks where strange old records may be puzzled out from half-obliterated inscriptions,—and companioned by the melancholy, dying palms, looks pensive and appealing. "The Pearl of Egypt" is no longer counted of such price as when pilgrims came flocking even from Greece and Italy for the mystic healing of Isis. Long after the rest of Egypt and Nubia had been Christianized by imperial edict, Osiris, the God of Suffering, Death and Resurrection, Isis, "Our Lady of Enchantments," and their son, Horus, in whose honor a sacred hawk was kept by the priests in the temple, were worshipped with the old "Osirian Mysteries" at Philae. We saw one solitary hawk sailing slowly over from the barren, desolate hills of the bank, with its debris of rocks, and circling above his ancient shrine. All those capitals and heads of broken columns, those cornices and edges of wall, peering above the water, were, like the pylons and kiosk, of a soft brown color that turned golden in the sun. Under the pale-blue, misted sky the whole scene was sad, and yet perhaps more beautiful for that very sadness. The submerged temple seemed symbolic of the old faith overflowed by new and stranger tides of life.

After the two months in Egypt the party embarked for Palestine:

First View of the Holy Land

Faint in the pearly dawn, a silver line
It gleamed upon the sea; our hearts were there
Before our vision, your dear heart and mine,
And every face about us was a prayer.

More than any other experience Katharine hoped to bring this pilgrimage to her mother and all those she cared for deeply. She wrote a "Palestine Chronicle" for publication, in part only, in the *Wellesley Magazine*. To her mother she sent her more intimate descriptions. The account of her visits to the mountain popularly believed to have been the scene of the Sermon on the Mount characteristically mingles reverence, keen observation, and humor:

A few miles before reaching the edge of the plateau which falls a thousand feet to the Sea of Galilee we had passed, the day before, the Horns of Hattin, known to pilgrims as the Mount of the Beatitudes. It was the scene of the crucial defeat of the Crusaders by Saladin, but its supreme interest lies in the fact that, whether or no it was the amphitheatre of the Sermon on the Mount, it must have been known to Him who so loved to withdraw into mountain solitude for rest and prayer. It is only sixty feet high, with a long summit rising into the "horns" at either end. I wanted to climb it, and Hashem was downcast at the proposal. "It is never done, my lady," he protested. "I have been dragoman ten time, and I never do it." But when he found I was trying to arrange for another guide, he yielded the point with his usual gentle submission to the inscrutable will of Allah. "If we must do it, we must do it," he said sadly, and ordered our wagon and horses for one o'clock. So the young driver and Hashem and the three horses and I—five creatures made gloomy by the persistency of one—jogged up the steep side of the plateau again, worked our way along the miry track for a while and then turned off into the fields, the driver bringing us as near the hill as he could. We were within a mile of the Mount when we finally left our cart, and I abandoned my coat, but took my stout umbrella for a staff, and Hashem, with a thick stick of his own, resignedly led the way, consoling himself with a succession of cigarettes, flat against the precepts of Mohammed. The only trouble about the walk was the heat, and the fact that the grass and weeds and thistles hid the rolling stones with which all Palestine is strewn as thick as pepper. Among these stones wild flowers were growing freely,—clover, daisies, yellow mustard, and the beautiful red anemone which is believed to be Christ's "lily of the field." The climb was not hard, though Hashem helped me over the crags, intermingled with loose rock, that framed the summit. Once arrived, it was a place of perfect repose and beauty, a long, slightly hollowed reach of soft turf, abounding in blue iris, with two enclosed wells, and some few foundation stones of a perished home or church. On the west rose the long range of Mount Carmel—twelve miles of level height. Well might Amos say that "the habitations of the shepherds shall mourn," when "the top of Carmel shall wither." On the east I could see the blue, shining lake of Galilee, as long as Carmel, and note the inlet of the Jordan on the north and, more distinctly, the valley of its outlet on the south. The green cone of Tabor rose on the south-west, and beyond it the broken line of the Samaritan mountains. Conspicuous in the north is Safed, now a "city set on a hill" which "cannot be hid," but it is not certain that there was a city here in the time of Christ.

I wanted to read the Sermon on the Mount here, but Hashem was tramping disconsolately about and urging the descent. As a guide, he pointed out the black tents of the Bedouins in the sloping pastures below and said it would never do to let the dusk find us in their neighborhood; as a philosopher, he opined that the Bible could be read anywhere else as well as here and was no better worth reading anywhere than the Koran,—"It all the same: if man read good words in one book or one other book, and follow, all right; if not follow, not all right"; as a friend, he expressed concern for my cold, which would not be bettered by my sitting down, without my coat on on a breezy summit after a hot climb.

So I contented myself with the Beatitudes, while Hashem, afraid I would read them aloud, edged off as far as possible under excuse of gathering a posy of the iris blossoms for Miss Hazard. Alas! they were exquisite as they swayed amid the grasses, but they were closed and perished before we got them home, and the few I pressed only left a blue stain on the page. It is so with any effort to tell you what that peaceful summit, so accessible on the one side to the fishers from the lake and on the other to the shepherds from the hills, meant to me. It is almost certain that Christ loved that beautiful refuge and was often there, looking out on the same views of hill and plain and water, touching just such lovely blossoms with His sandaled feet. I wanted to remain for hours, but I meekly followed Hashem, who took a tight grip of my arm and hurried me down the stony hillside, of rather uncertain foothold, into the plain. As we were coming out into the miry track again, the driver suddenly pointed out to me two light little creatures leaping away at a distance over the tops of the tall dry thistles,—wild gazelles, that seemed to be nothing but color and motion, so airy and swift they were. The horses frisked for joy when they found they were going back down hill to Tiberias and started off at such a pace that we reached the inn soon after six.

As Katharine and her companions left the Holy Land she closed a final letter: "We are homesick already, as I think we shall always be in our hearts, for the lake and the hills Christ loved." She wrote her last reverent quatrains of the pilgrimage. One, "At Gethsemane," is especially poignant and moving:

There is a sighing in the pallid sprays
Of these old olives, as if still they kept
Their pitying watch, in Nature's faithful ways,
As on that night when the disciples slept.

At Naples Miss Hazard and Katharine parted, planning to meet in London later. Katharine hurried to the International Institute in Madrid to attend important directors' meetings. After two weeks in Spain she joined Miss Scoville and others for several weeks of rest in Italy and Switzerland. She wrote a gay letter to her mother from Grindelwald in July, 1907:

Nan is as indignant with me for writing about Palestine in Switzerland as Miss Hazard was grieved at my writing about England in Egypt. "When you get to Heaven," says Nan, "you'll have no time to walk the golden streets, or learn to sing,—and you'll have to *learn* if you're to be in the choir—or, least of all, to get your crown and wings fitted. You'll just sit down in your own mansion to write a history of the *earth*."

We have walked down the Rigi and were stiff and foot-blistered and queer in our ears. Nan has been wild to "climb all the views" and has longed for fiercer Alps. So we came on here, jumping off at Lauterbrunnen. We walked to a famous waterfall, and over the Wengern Alp. Just as we were up there, over 7,000 feet above sea-level, right against the mighty snowfront of the Jungfrau, the thunder broke upon us like her own voice, and the lightning leaped all about us, while hail came crashing down. But presently we passed out above the storm into a region where new powdery snow lay on this lovely multitude of Alpine flowers. How I wish that you were here to rejoice in them! I need not mention that I am feeling better!

By mid-July she had returned to London. After a few weeks of intensive work at the British Museum and the Bodleian, she returned in late August to Wellesley and her own brown-shingled home on Curve Street.

XIX

"Scarab"

KATHARINE'S family gathered in Wellesley to welcome her home, to admire the new house, and to take over many of the tiresome details of furnishing and moving. In a few days the house took on a comfortable and charming aspect. To entertain his mother and sisters, Arthur equipped several window-sills with feeding trays for birds and set up a little whirling weather-vane, a ridiculous small sailor who was at once named for Clement, the ancestor who had been the first to come across the sea. Cherishing the goal of peace in an intimate atmosphere of her own creating, Katharine cheerfully set about housekeeping, smiling under "the tyranny of things," and grateful to all who helped her in the confusion of minor crises.

At last the house was habitable, and out of her full trunk came the souvenirs of the travel year: the bright beads, the pictures of Egyptian kings and queens, the small antiquities, meaningful regardless of value, the embroideries, the alabaster, and the little lamp from Nazareth. All the new mementos were added to older treasures to create the charm of the "Scarab's" rooms.

True to her practice of bestowing her own names on people and places, she had chosen the name for her home while she was in Egypt. The fabled beetle of the Nile and the Mediterranean shores had caught her imagination. Drawn as a hieroglyph it acquired a symbolic significance as the sign for the

Egyptian verb which means "become" or, perhaps, "create." There could be no better name for Katharine's house than the "Scarab," and a small scarab of dull green stone was placed under the study mantel. The little stone wing of Truth, bought in Luxor, was also placed there, and in the hearth was set a tile given to her by a friend in the hope that its armored knight, who charged toward the study door with lance poised, would forever ward off all cares and griefs.

The furnishings of the house were simple but comfortable. The warm red Bokhara, Miss Hazard's gift, gave the study color and beauty, and the blue tiles, on which small ships sailed home to port, framed the fireplace of another room and gave it the name "The Haven." The countless books lent their color to the rooms from behind the glass doors of tall bookcases bought in second-hand stores to match the old mahogany case in which Katharine's grandfather and father had kept their books and sermons.

Although the Scarab "bit" during the settling, gradually it began to seem like home. Mrs. Bates and Jeannie moved into their sunny corner rooms and Katharine into her bedroom and study. Each of these rooms had a screened porch, one for sleeping and one for working outdoors when the weather permitted. On the third floor a large room had been finished for Katharine Coman, who soon arrived, bringing Sigurd, their collie, who had been a most important member of the family for the last four years.

Katharine took up the year's work at Wellesley with her usual anticipation. Her relatives soon departed, and the family settled down to routine. Katharine's Tuesday "at home," which had begun a few years earlier, continued, and the seminar gathered once more. While Katharine went about her daily occupations, Mrs. Bates did the family sewing and worked on a translation from the Spanish of Gustavo Becquer's short stories, which she and Katharine planned to publish.

Jeannie presided over the domestic affairs, typed manuscripts, or worked at the delicate water-color paintings for the personal Christmas cards it had become Katharine's custom to send. The two Katharines usually found time for an evening walk with Sigurd, who often accompanied them to the campus, lying on guard outside the office or classroom door.

The fall and early winter of 1907 were "most beautiful." The Thanksgiving and Christmas holidays seemed to consecrate the new home at last. Not until after the new year was it realized that sorrow was drawing near. A sudden illness overcame Mrs. Bates, and in late January, 1908, the rose-colored room stood empty. The journey was made back to Falmouth and the familiar cemetery. Village friends were waiting with all the old love and neighborliness. Katharine found a deep sense of comfort in being with Hattie Gifford, the oldest of her friends.

For Katharine the new house now seemed purposeless, but she sought to fill the emptiness in her heart by writing for the family an intimate account of the last months of her mother's life and by working on the Becquer tales, which were published under the title *Romantic Legends of Spain* the following year. Mrs. Bates and Katharine had intended to dedicate the work to Jeannie, but it was inscribed instead, by the wish of both daughters, to "a shining memory."

Gustavo Adolfo Becquer, who was best known as a poet, was considered by many to be the most original literary figure in Spain in the nineteenth century. His prose was little recognized abroad, since, as Katharine said in a note to the introduction, with the exception of "a few waifs and strays, usually in abridged form, and for seven out of the twelve stories in W. W. Gibbings' 'Terrible Tales,' these legends have not before been translated into English." The volume contained twenty-one pieces, nearly all characterized as tales or legends, and was immediately welcomed as an important contribution to literature, written in a style which faithfully mirrored the spirit and personality of the brilliant Spaniard who had died before his genius, which was akin to Poe's, had received full recognition.

But Katharine's mother was not there to enjoy the praise, to read the reviews, and to sniff with characteristic skepticism at the superlatives. Such pleasure as Katharine had in the publication lay in the completion of the work for the chief translator, the finishing for her mother of a happy task.

During the sorrowful winter while Miss Coman was absent on leave, Katharine was especially sustained and comforted by Miss Hazard, whose "sweet and quiet friendship" often beguiled her to a restful week end at Miss Hazard's home in Peace Dale, Rhode Island. Here, with Miss Hazard, Katharine received Holy Communion for the first time. Thereafter she was often a communicant in Peace Dale and in Wellesley. Understanding thoroughly the significances and values of corporate worship, she took her place many times with congregations in both Protestant and Catholic churches, loving the traditions and the ancient rites, but still missing, as she wrote, her "Christ of the Silence."

Katharine had a deep reverence for tradition and recognized the appeal of orthodox religious practices which had been so strong in her family. But her close friends knew that she instinctively moved steadily away from Catholic positions in the direction of the spiritual life as Masefield understood it, "all imagined or apprehended Life," not a "rule of sanctity or austerity." What she had seen and heard in Spain, what she knew of the attitudes of members of the Church of England, who, clinging to the doctrine of apostolic succession, could recognize none but Catholic communions, repelled her. All her life she was a student of the New Testament. She found no justification in any words of Christ for the exclusivism which she had encountered in its cruelest modern aspects and had witnessed with the deepest abhorrence. As Marion Pelton Guild said of her, the supreme figure of Christ was her Leader and her Lord. Most humbly she sought to follow the all-embracing religion of Love which she had early chosen and which she believed Christ came to earth to preach.

The skepticism of those who regarded the New Testament story as myth was repugnant to her. The loving, compassionate words, "Father, forgive them, for they know not what they do," were the supreme proof, for, she asked, "What mythmaker could invent them?" The divinity of Christ she never questioned. Divinity was implicit in His every word and act. He had drawn the breath of divinity from the spirit of Love "in whom eternal Godhood dwells." She needed no proof in dogma. Dogma was the business of theologians. Divinity, "overspread and cast abroad upon the whole earth and universe," pressed in upon her overwhelmingly and was revealed in the life and words of Christ, who said, "A new commandment I give unto you, that ye love one another; as I have loved you, that ye also love one another. By this shall all men know that ye are my disciples, if ye have love one to another."

It would always be the awareness of divinity for which she searched in all her reading and study, and she returned again and again to the great writers in whom this awareness shone. Among her countrymen Emerson, of course, spoke most intimately to her. The young Jonathan Edwards, before he was overtaken by Calvinistic theology, was of the company, as were Whittier, William Vaughn Moody, Emily Dickinson to whom "the world of sense was almost transparent," Sophie Jewett, and many another. She found what she sought in Vaughan, Traherne, Wordsworth, and Bridges. Among the spiritual searchings which she greatly valued were *Marius the Epicurean* and *John Inglesant*. Christina Rossetti was her chosen poet, and she knew more than fifty of her poems by heart. It was Christina's collected poems and the worn volume of *Prayers Ancient and Modern* which she and Katharine Coman read most often. Her faint pencil marks were drawn beside those poems of Christina's in which the word "hope" appears. With her, she cherished "a wondering love that hopes and hails Thy boundless Love of me."

If their mother's death was a bereavement for Katharine, it was an overwhelming loss for Jeannie. For many years her mother's constant companion and, as Mrs. Bates grew older, her most loving and devoted attendant, she was now inexpressibly lonely. In their grief the sisters drew closer to each other. The care that had been lavished upon her mother Jeannie now expended on Katharine, seeking to relieve her of every material and domestic problem. Katharine, mindful of the isolation of the deaf, drew Jeannie into her own full life in every possible way. Jeannie's constant endeavor was to overcome her infirmity so that it would cause her sister no anxiety or extra effort on her behalf. She studied lip-reading and became so skillful that conversation with her was not too difficult, and she followed easily most of the dinner-table talk. The sisters were seldom alone, for all the available rooms were occupied by graduate students, who counted it a privilege to live at the "Scarab." Jeannie established a routine in the home and spent her time typing and decorating not only her sister's cards but other designs sent to her. "Miss Jeannie," as she was widely known in the village, was a gay little person, short and stout, with bright brown eyes behind gold-rimmed glasses. She betrayed no bitterness, and rarely even wistfulness, because of her handicap and her financial dependence. But a dignified and rather pathetic little note Katharine found after her death gave some evidence of the disappointments and heartaches she had concealed. She made her sociable rounds on the family errands and was acquainted with many a friendly "gossip," with whom she paused to exchange the news of the day.

Evening invariably found Jeannie seated on her favorite bench in the wide hall reading the *Transcript,* Sigurd curled up near her in his own leather Sleepy Hollow chair, both aware of every vibration within the house and ready to greet or serve those who entered. Katharine became very dependent upon her, and her journal records heartfelt appreciation of every service, especially of the warm and loving welcome at each day's end.

XX

Loneliness

WRITING AND EDITING for children was a special field which had always attracted Katharine. Scandinavian literature held a fascination for her, and she often gave *Sigurd the Volsung* to her young friends. She had particularly enjoyed editing a collection of stories from Norse mythology by Hamilton Wright Mabie. Her interest in the northern legends persisted all her life. Other books she gave regularly to children were *Master Skylark* and *Will Shakespeare's Little Lad.* She herself wrote many short stories and poems for children and assumed the general supervision of "The Canterbury Classics," a series of supplementary readers. She contributed to the series a simplified version of Chaucer's *Canterbury Tales.* She did not attempt to render the original text in any literal sense but followed Chaucer's lines as much as possible and at the same time simplified phrases and omitted allusions beyond the understanding of a child. For three of the tales she used the versions of Dryden, Wordsworth, and Leigh Hunt. Her fine scholarship and literary skill were in evidence throughout the book, touched with a freshness that pleased the reviewers. The little volume was dedicated to Wallace Hamilton, the young son of Professor Hamilton who had composed the setting for "America the Beautiful."

Wallace was one of her best-loved playmates. When he decided to assume the character of Sherlock Holmes, Katharine immediately took the role of Ebenezer Gryce, and much mysterious detecting followed. It was a relationship that was typical of her happy friendships with children. One of her letters to Wallace gives the flavor of these gay interludes in her busy days:

Aug. 17, 1909

My dear Mr. Holmes,—

or may I not, in consideration of our long intercourse in detecting the crimes of our betters, say—

My dear Sher:

I thank you, and I thank your dear mother, for the birthday condolences which helped me through the arch of years looking out on the western horizon. When I came to the breakfast table that morning, I found K.L.B. inscribed upon it in fifty shining new cents. Soon arrived fifty carnations from Mrs. Guild. And a flat, soft package, which I had accepted from Miss Scofield the evening before, innocently believing it, after various detective punches to be a scarf or half-dozen handkerchiefs, turned out fifty dollar bills. So I had various reminders of the number of strides Time has made—poor Gaffer Time—since he set me up on his shoulder. Some day he'll get tired and drop me hard—that's his rude way. But I have been leading such a riotous life, since attaining these years of indiscretion, that you would hardly know your desk-loving partner. My nephew and his mother are here, and we have trolleyed and trained and driven and sailed, and today we give a Yellow Tea in commemoration of the fact that Sigurd will be seven years old next Friday. As my guests, and my sister with them, go to Portland tomorrow, we have to hurry up his date a bit. Little Percy Wood brought him over a beautiful wreath of goldenrod last night. My sister-in-law said, when I finally arrayed him in it, that he looked like the golden calf,—which has occasioned a family coolness. The sun has refused to come to his Yellow Tea, but I think we shall make out very well without him, as the (tissue paper) table linen, cakes, drinks, candies and all are yellow. I wish you could all come.

I don't see why you and Semi-Captain Elwood can't put a flying attachment onto your mail steamer and drop in at Camp Scarab. I'm glad you are having such a good time—free for the moment from the crushing weight of our professional cares—and with love to your juvenile parents, I'm

Gryce

(May I not say 'Sneezer!)

The variety of Katharine's literary work was stimulating but taxing. Requests came more and more often for reviews, for special articles, for occasional poems, for editing, for introductions. She could not undertake all the tasks but chose those for which she felt best qualified. She was happier in more spontaneous creative work. She had slowly gathered and arranged the poems which she felt possessed some merit, and these were published in 1911 in the volume *America the Beautiful,* which she called a "mere budget of life." The critics were even more generous in their praise of her poetry than of her prose. At the time they placed her in the foremost rank of American women poets. It was considered that her poetry was of a high order and indicated a wide range of scholarship, human feeling, nobility of tone, and tenderness of imagination. Her understanding of the hidden and subtle experiences of life was revealed in poem after poem.

The single poem most often mentioned was the "Threnody" written for Sophie Jewett, Katharine's associate in the department for twenty years. Miss Jewett's "discernment, her wholesome strength, her comprehension, and her faith" had been unfailing in her companionship with Katharine. Poets and teachers alike, they were always in sympathy with one another's highest purposes. Katharine had depended greatly upon her friend's understanding and support. After Miss

Jewett's death the department was never quite the same. Katharine found a measure of comfort in preparing for the press Miss Jewett's English versions of *Folk Ballads of Southern Europe* and her edition of De Amicis' *Cuore*, thus making her contribution to the lasting reputation of a fine scholar, whose modern version of *The Pearl*, dedicated to Katharine, had just been published.

Katharine omitted many of the poems in *America the Beautiful* from later collections, but she was never sufficiently ruthless in her critical judgment of her own poetry. Her mail gave ample evidence of the comfort or pleasure her poems brought to many readers, and she could do no less than share with them her own sense of joy and beauty, and love, "earth's one divinest word." Later it was difficult to discard such poems. Her slightest work was effortless and so much a part of her being that the poems almost seemed to write themselves. Miss Scudder, writing after her death, said, "I marvel at the variety of rhythm, the perfectness of rhyme, the unfailing beat. Hers was indeed a singing soul; I can hardly imagine what it must be like so to have one's inner consciousness constantly ripple as hers must have done, in melody."

At about this time she wrote a story for children, *In Sunny Spain*, for the "Little Schoolmate" series, which was published under the general editorship of Florence Converse. Her intimate and sympathetic knowledge of Spain enriched the little story, which was a blend of fact and fancy.

No matter how wide the divergence between Katharine's occupations and interests and those of her friends, she was always aware of their accomplishments, their activities, and their opinions. She understood and shared each one's thoughts to a marked degree, but kept her own independence and followed her own beliefs, which were controlled and reasoned. She was keenly interested in the socialism of several of her intimates, although she was not in agreement with socialist theory. Some of her opinions upon this subject are expressed in a letter written after attending a socialist meeting in Boston which had been addressed by a colleague on the Wellesley faculty:

Miss Hayes, who presided, was really charming and, from the first, had that great audience in her pocket. She bore herself with quiet dignity and looked impressive and attractive in her plain blue suit, with her gray hair crowning a face that wore, for all its quietness, a look of exaltation and unembarrassed content. Her comrades gave her a mighty ovation and three times the roll of applause died down and flooded in again before she could get a chance to begin. Her brief address was written. It told the story of Runnymede and then arraigned modern Capitalism, very cleverly and humorously, under the name of King John. She made frank reference to Ettor and set the house off with a tumult of applause. She asked me, coming home, what I thought of it all and, having said the many pleasant things that I could very cordially say, I protested against her intensifying class hatred and calling out class antagonism. I told her that, as it seemed to me, this meeting, whose concern was with socialism as a theory of society to be tested by the vote, was a very different matter from the meeting at Lawrence, where law and order were in jeopardy, but even here I didn't like to hear her arraign the rich, whereas I did like to hear Keir Hardie tell the workers what they, themselves, as workers and voters and socialists, ought to do. He was admirable in every way,—eloquent, mellow, speaking as one who had faith in all humanity and not merely in factory hands and miners, showing the workers that they had only to vote for socialist reforms, which was just what in the United States they had hardly begun to do, and distinctly warning them against spending constructive energy in scolding.

Katharine's familiar routine of teaching, writing, domesticity, and public duties was happily interrupted from time to time by short journeys, brief lecture tours, and motor trips with Miss Hazard through the Berkshires, the Taconics, and the long mountain ranges of Vermont and New Hampshire. There were summer engagements at the Bread Loaf Summer School, where she lectured on six of Shakespeare's plays, assisted by Miss Scoville. There she rejoiced in the mountain peace and the congenial literary atmosphere. She made occasional summer trips to Europe which were designed more for work than for recreation. In July, 1913, she left with Katharine Coman for her third sabbatical leave and her last foreign journey.

It was a year of accomplishment with an undercurrent of anxiety about Miss Coman, who had undergone two serious operations in the years just past. Katharine, fearing for her friend's health and strength, was none too well herself. A consultation with physicians had resulted in an ultimatum: she must have complete rest and change. Miss Coman's journey already had been planned with a friend and colleague Olga Halsey along the lines of her special interests. To join Miss Coman and Miss Halsey seemed the obvious solution. The two Katharines were long accustomed to adjusting their diverse research projects and literary labors. Miss Coman had retired from teaching and was devoting all her time to writing. Her chief interest lay in economic studies, and her two important works in this field were the *Industrial History of the United States* and *Economic Beginnings of the Far West.*

The first country visited that summer was Norway. Katharine lay on her balcony at the hotel at Christiania, resting, reading proofs, and writing, regaining her strength while her companions traveled about in Sweden investigating social-insurance problems. Katharine called her own employment "cultivating the fine, almost forgotten art of loafing." She had no knack for real idleness, and she felt that she had been well since her first hour at sea. But mindful of doctors' orders, she relaxed in her new surroundings and wrote the lyrics of this northern vacation.

The year's plans included six months in Spain preceded by two months in England for Katharine, while her friends traveled and studied on the Continent. The arrangement gave her time to take up again her research for the edition of the Heywood plays which had been so long deferred. She studied Spanish intensively to prepare herself for teaching and lecturing duties at the Institute in the winter.

In Spain Miss Coman continued her own work and seemed to regain health steadily. She was able to share in the life of the Institute and to travel widely with Katharine, who was again devoting much time to cathedrals and Catholic services. The months in Spain ended with a leisurely vacation-journey up the coast to Paris where the friends separated, Katharine going to London to conclude the Heywood study. When Katharine Coman rejoined her, word came of the death of Sigurd, their companion for twelve years.

In spite of the encouraging signs in regard to Miss Coman's health, she was weak and ill when she arrived from Paris, and alarming indications of a serious condition appeared almost immediately. An appointment was made with a London physician who, after a second examination, reversed his first and favorable opinion and gave a definite and ominous verdict. Miss Coman had only a few months to live. With quiet grace and steadfast courage she canceled her plans to work in Germany and to participate in two European conferences. Katharine, still hoping for a contradiction of the medical opinion when they should reach New York, packed hastily and wound up their European affairs, stifling her despair and trying to match Miss Coman's serenity and poise. They spoke often of Sigurd. To Katharine's anxious mind, his death was almost a portent. On walks with his two mistresses it had been his habit to run ahead to "find the path." Had he gone once more to seek out the way for the one he loved best?

They sailed for home in mid-June. Katharine, who felt herself the weaker of the two in many ways, kept her dread and sorrow concealed. Miss Coman was strong in faith and had no fear of death. She shrank from the coming months only because of the burden of pain and sorrow they would bring to those she loved.

No real hope was held out that her life could continue for long, but, looking upon earthly life as only a phase of eternal life, she faced the temporary separation from family and friends with composure. Only once did Katharine see a trace of tears in her eyes at the thought of parting from all that she had known and loved. She spent the summer in the Berkshires under ideal conditions. Katharine was with her, sharing with Emily Balch, their close friend, the summer days that slipped quickly away. With the coming of autumn Miss Coman returned to "Bohemia," the wide room in the Scarab where the windows looked out to the treetops and the sky.

Katharine carried on her accustomed tasks but spent every free moment with Miss Coman, who, for a time, was able to work on an industrial history of New England and enjoy family life. But the weeks were all too short, and in January, 1914, Katharine sat at Miss Coman's bedside, repeating lines they both loved. She leaned near to repeat, "Underneath are the everlasting arms," before the last breath was quietly drawn.

In those first days, "bewildered past all pain, past all desire," in grief "too dull for tears," Katharine went about the necessary tasks, carrying out Miss Coman's wishes, and then took up a life empty of a comradeship of thirty-five years. She asked no healing for her sorrow, accepting the suffering of her personal loss, which was constant and profound in all the years remaining to her. Much earlier in their friendship she had written about Miss Coman:

May God who wrought our fleeting race
Forbid her fatal star,
Remembering she is the grace
Of all that are.

That prayer had gone unanswered. The haunting fear of the withdrawal of human companionship had been realized. The silence which she had felt in all previous losses with an intense awareness, and which had led her to choose Hamlet's dying words, "The rest is silence," for the title of three sonnets written after her mother's death, now closed about her. As Miss Coman would have wished, she tried to turn her mind from the remembered living aspect of her friend and sought to rejoice in the deliverance which she, too, would experience. She was sustained by sentences from one of Miss Coman's last notes to her: "I have no fear, Dear Heart, for Life and Death are one, and God is all in all. My only real concern to remain in this body is to spare you pain and grief and loneliness. But I should not leave you comfortless. I would come to you as my mother comes to me in my best moments when my heart is open to her. The breezes come in off the meadow where the song sparrows are piping. Surely God is love."

Now, with the old longing for some intimation of a world beyond the veiled and groping understanding of mortals intensified and deepened, she lived more and more an inner life of the spirit. Yet she did not wholly withdraw from her friends. Writing to a member of Miss Coman's family, she shared the wisdom won by hard experience: "I seem to find Katharine again, not in vision, but within myself, the courage in my grief, the comfort in my weariness, and the guidance in my perplexity. We must not cease loving and working, we who sorrow, for our Beloveds are pressing on in bright new paths of service, and it will never do for us to be left too far behind. A teacher of mine said to her husband: 'Don't live one negative day for the sake of grief. I expect to go on and on. You must keep up with me, one doing God's will in one place and one in another.' It is hard to lose the mortal life but sooner or later, all love has to pass from body to spirit—from the joy of touch and sight and hearing to the inner communion."

Katharine was held to her "reasonable hope" by the integrity of her soul. She believed it to be a better and more helpful desire than the desire for absolute knowledge. Such desire could lead one to an acceptance in which self-deception might play a part. This, for her, would mean a disloyalty to Truth, which is beyond the grasp of the finite mind. She saw and recognized law in the universe. She could believe that there was a will within the law. She could believe Love to be that will. She had asked, "How does Love come, unless Love is?"—and Love was manifest. She wrote of "this vast incertitude . . . our immensity of doubt." But to "Will within the Law, and Love that Will," she lifted a "faltering faith," longing for the sure faith that had sustained Miss Coman, but unable to be false to her own Truth. If intensity of hope such as hers may become faith, then slowly she may have attained it. But her poems do not reveal it, although many correspondents wrote that they felt a sense of faith in one or another poem.

In the first lonely months Katharine went often to Cornelia Warren's estate, "Cedar Hill," in Waltham. Miss Warren and Miss Coman had been intimate friends, sharing an interest in the development of the settlement house. Miss Coman's interest in this work dated from the early days of Hull House and her friendship with Jane Addams. Katharine Bates took no active part in this movement, but she did have a general interest in the formation of the College Settlement Association, of which Miss Coman had been president for a number of years. Miss Coman had gone to "Cedar Hill" to convalesce from operations, and Miss Warren had established an additional tie when she gave Sigurd to the two Katharines.

She disapproved of their choice, for Sigurd had been appointed her barn dog since he lacked show points. For that reason he was, of course, the very dog they took to their hearts. In this period of adjustment in Katharine's life, Miss Warren often took her away to the peace of her country estate and thoughtfully included Jeannie in her invitations.

Helped immeasurably by her sister's love and by the sympathy of her friends, Katharine slowly resumed her many tasks and obligations, finding comfort in familiar routines and peace in Miss Coman's "Bohemia," which she now took for her own room. Here, at her friend's desk by a south window, she wrote the poems of the later period of her life.

XXI

The World of Wellesley

KATHARINE had relied upon Miss Coman's calm strength of character even more than she had realized. In the months following her friend's death she found adjustment to life without her an almost impossible task. She wrote to a friend some months later, "I miss her more and more, and yet, sometimes—But put these impressions into words and they are gone."

Her friends drew closer to her. Cora Scofield, Emily Balch, and Olga Halsey, who had been Miss Coman's close friends, joined earlier comrades, Miss Scudder, Miss Sherwood, and others. These women often gathered at the Scarab to talk around the study fire. Although Miss Hazard had retired from the presidency, no break had occurred in her close friendship with Katharine. She came frequently to the college guest house and often took Katharine with her to Peace Dale. Miss Scoville wrote to her, "I have a soul that needs care and it is a long time since you have shepherded me." Slowly she was made to feel how much she was needed.

The great fire at Wellesley, which had occurred while Katharine and Miss Coman were in Spain, had destroyed College Hall and left the school with many adjustments and anxieties. Katharine must take her share with others in the work of reconstruction and the task of raising money. With pride she watched her friend Ellen Fitz Pendleton, now Wellesley's president, going courageously ahead with the complicated administration of a college which must literally be built anew. Katharine had rejoiced that Wellesley had found in one of her own daughters the fortunate combination of talents that fitted her admirably for the presidency. But despite all Miss Pendleton's fine abilities, one of Wellesley's professors remarked with a twinkle of her eyes that "Nellie Pen" was always, of course, properly subordinate to the older alumnae. Miss Pendleton had always turned to Katharine for advice. Her older friend's long association with the college, her careful thinking and considered opinions had made her something of an elder statesman in the administration of the college. At this time Miss Pendleton sought her counsel, and came to the Scarab for long talks about the future as well as immediate problems. "Nellie Pen" to her friends and "Pres. Pen" to her girls, she was Wellesley's outstanding leader in that dark hour, and Katharine, proud to see her friend's powers grow, put aside her personal tragedy and exerted herself for Miss Pendleton and the college. To those watching in that early March dawn it must have seemed as if the college itself were crashing down, destroyed with the falling brick and mortar. But when the hour for morning chapel came, Miss Pendleton announced that classes would be held on the appointed date after the spring vacation which was about to begin. Before the day ended, Bishop Lawrence, president of the board of trustees, called on Miss Pendleton to help lay the groundwork for the tremendous effort ahead. In her book *Wellesley College* Florence Converse wrote, "Two hundred and sixteen people were houseless; the departments of Zoology, Geology, Physics, and Psychology, had lost their laboratories, their equipment, their lecture rooms: twenty-eight recitation rooms, all the administrative offices, the offices of twenty departments, the assembly hall, the study hall, had all been swept away." But there remained the chapel, the library, the art building, the chemistry building, the observatory, the botany laboratory, the music hall, the gymnasium, the dormitories, and the college hospital. To these was soon added a sprawling one-story wooden building, which, while Wellesley was being rebuilt, became the heart of the college.

The challenge to all Wellesley women roused Katharine to an intensity of effort. She had known the college when it came into being, and in its rebirth she saw again the old vision, "the dream within the deed." What she had written of Oxford she felt as deeply of Wellesley: "The unending life of human thought is here, enduring, achieving, advancing, with its constant miracle of resurrection out of the old form into the new."

In reviewing Miss Converse's book she wrote, "Of this essential Wellesley there are many builders, from the clergymen in our pulpit to the leaders of Student Government meetings. A steady hammering comes from the executive offices, from the Academic Council and from departments. Sparks fly, sometimes, and often we workers are blinded by our own dust. . . . What would the daughters of Wellesley, now in their maturity of wisdom, have her do, have her be? We do not answer hastily, for if perishable stone must be shaped with care, how much more imperishable thought! But our answer, when it finally comes, will not be a timid one. We will not be afraid of horizon spaces nor of starry goals. Whatever her children ask of her Wellesley will attain, whatever they foretell for her, Wellesley will fulfil; her greatness grows with the greatness of our love,—a love which has become power. The story of Wellesley is only just begun."

It did not fall to Katharine to meet bereavement alone and with idle hands. The world of Wellesley drew her inexorably, and beyond it the European war darkened all minds and dwarfed all personal catastrophe.

The Wellesley world was essentially the student world, and the girls were constantly with her, both in and out of the classroom. With the opening of the college year Katharine identified each of them in her own way. In her record book she wrote private reminders: "She wears her yellow hair in three puffs. . . . Her grandmother has a parrot. . . . She has been to Elsinore. . . . Notre Dame is her favorite cathedral. . . . She has a twin brother at Harvard." The girls alone would have filled her life. They flocked to the Scarab and sought her out as a mother confessor. Home troubles, love affairs, aspirations, hidden faults—all were poured out by the study fire. To many, in after years, their beloved "'Fessor" was the symbol of all that Wellesley had meant.

Katharine also had an immediate part to play in the social life of the campus and the town. Her acceptance of the various circles in which she lived was characteristic of her. Never aloof, she found a place in neighborly village activities or in literary groups in Boston and was at home in all her worlds.

Not long before Katharine's last sabbatical leave, to her infinite comfort and joy Mrs. Mary Reddell had come to her household as housekeeper and friend, bringing with her a little daughter. Mrs. Guild believed that, as the years went by, Mrs. Reddell developed an intuitive understanding of Katharine which surpassed that of any other person. With one brief interlude she remained at the Scarab as long as Katharine lived. Her presence in the house created an atmosphere of peace and order. Katharine, who called her "the homemaker," could scarcely imagine life without her, and was always soothed and rested by her soft, musical voice and gentle ways, her anticipation of every want, and her thoughtful, loving care of the family to whom she became a "steadfast saint" and a "ministering angel."

Katharine slowly took up her literary work again. The Heywood plays were published in the "Belles Lettres Series." This, her most scholarly work, attracted little general notice but brought appreciative letters from colleagues whose interests centered in the English drama of the sixteenth and seventeenth centuries. Late in her life she said, speaking of this edition, "With that volume I but touched the fringes of scholarship." She added, "And in three or four poems I have but touched the fringes of poetry." She wrote to a friend, "I have done only what under the limitations set around life I could; perhaps not that, not nearly that."

After completion of this work Katharine turned to a volume of verse for children, including poems on Christmas and nature, and writing a fairy play for the opening selection. The book was published under the title *Fairy Gold*.

Katharine's correspondence upon the subject of her hymn "America the Beautiful" had grown to monumental proportions. The poem, long known to "my disrespectful family" as "A. and B.," a nickname she happily adopted, acquired its own large cupboard. As the musical settings and the bundles of letters multiplied, proper care of the mass of papers became a formidable task. From time to time Arthur undertook the responsibility of keeping the cupboard in order. What fame had come to Katharine from this poem, which in letters to her family she often called "our hymn," she maintained was due to this brother, who had made many sacrifices that she might have an education. Not only the praise for this poem, but everything good that came to her in life, she attributed to the love and assistance of her family, and especially Arthur. A wide recognition was now hers, and from the academic world beyond her own college she had received the first formal accolade of scholarship in the degree of Doctor of Letters conferred by Middlebury College. She was happy to be called in the citation "a granddaughter of Middlebury," since she had always had an affection for the college her grandfather had served as president.

The close of the college year 1915 was tumultuous. The class of 1880 returned for its thirty-fifth reunion, and the New

England Poetry Club, of which Katharine was a founder, held its first meeting at just that time. Committee meetings were attendant upon the launching, and for all of these Katharine had to go to Boston. Mrs. Guild, who was always fully informed on Katharine's activities, wrote that "her wise policies and spirit of cordial fellowship were of great service in the development of the club life." Katharine later served the club as president, and was also a vice-president of the Boston Authors Club.

But vacation days came and with them a new interest in the form of a little collie puppy. A kennel owner not far from Wellesley had known of Sigurd's long and happy life at the Scarab. He telephoned Katharine and begged her to take the strange little dog, who behaved as if he had been badly frightened. Thinking of the glorious Sigurd, Katharine had felt that she could never again have a dog in her home. But the right approach was made at just the right time. An unhappy little creature needed her. She could not resist the appeal, and so Hamlet, who had seen a ghost, came to the Scarab to be won slowly to a haunted happiness of his own, which kept him close to the few he could bring himself to trust.

The long summer wore away, with needed rest and change provided by a vacation in Vermont and visits with Jeannie in Portland where there were now three little grandnieces. Katharine's life was narrowing, in the geographical sense. She was growing tired. She still continued her long walks, but the distant journeys she had once made easily now seemed exhausting to contemplate. More and more she remained at home by the fireside, in "Bohemia," or on the tree-shaded porches where she could watch the changing seasons and listen to the grosbeak and the oriole.

XXII

"The Splendor Bides Within"

IN THE YEARS after the college fire Katharine's life and thought centered increasingly in Wellesley. The English Literature Department occupied her heart and mind closely. She had welcomed to the faculty younger members from various universities and had, through her gracious direction, created a group which worked together in complete harmony. Nearly all of the teachers continued the departmental tradition of publishing either imaginative work or articles of scholarly research. Departmental meetings, held by Katharine's fireside, became festive occasions where wit and wisdom, poetry and satire held reign, especially on the lips of the older members, Miss Bates, Miss Scudder, and Miss Sherwood, who were heard with the utmost appreciation by the younger members.

All the activities of the campus were of interest to Katharine. From the early days when Wellesley had been what George Herbert Palmer had called "a rough sketch of a college," every development had been watched and studied. Organizations and publications in which she had played a part had come and gone, but one, Phi Sigma, the undergraduate society of which she had been a charter member, had survived. Her classmate Emily Norcross Newton always enjoyed telling the society how, after a conference with Wellesley's founder during which the formation of two societies had been decided upon, she, small and light and swift, had run from the meeting and had been first to reach Katie Bates and claim her for Phi Sigma. The fortunes of the society were always vital to her, and she was available to its members all her life, from "Tradition Night" each autumn to the June breakfast, helping with the toasts for a formal occasion, writing a prayer for vesper service, and lending a hand in any way she could.

With the completion of the edition of the Heywood plays Katharine's major scholarly work ended. She was thoroughly preoccupied with the college and everything connected with it. She continued to write critical articles upon request, but she undertook no full-length work or any important research. When she found opportunity, she wrote poetry and brought out a collection of short plays for children, *Little Robin Stay Behind*. The book, as one reviewer said, was not a volume for the disillusioned ten-year-old who knows there is no Santa Claus, but was rather for the imaginative child to whom just such a fanciful trifle would appeal. It brought Katharine many letters from people who wrote to describe the pleasure children found in staging and acting the plays.

Mr. Bradford, always quick to send his appreciation of his friend's work, wrote: "I was much delighted with the volume of little plays. There is a wonderful freshness and grace and spirit about them. It seems as if the winds and waters and flowers frolicked all through the pages. And the rhymes are enchanting. It quite brings back to me the Ben Jonson masques,

> *Buzz, quoth the Blue-Fly,*
> *Hum, quoth the Bee.*

And there is a flavor of the old moralities in it too."

Although Katharine no longer traveled far afield, she experienced no sense of isolation. The world beyond Wellesley now came to her. Her correspondence became more of a problem every year. People wrote to ask for poems in her own handwriting, for autographs, for money, for advice, for study outlines, for estimates of the literature of all countries, for criticism of poems, for information on books in which certain literary characters might be found, and for political opinions.

Another academic honor came to Katharine in 1916, when Oberlin conferred upon her the degree of Doctor of Literature. She wrote to Arthur describing the event:

June 24, 1916

My dear Brother:

At last "the tumult and the shouting dies, the captains and the kings depart," both my Commencements are over, I have written belated letters to my Oberlin hosts, and my very next concern in life is to write to you, whose great kindness relieved me of the financial strain anticipated.

Do you want to hear about the trip?

I left a rainy Boston late on a Monday afternoon, had a cool and pleasant journey and reached Oberlin about two o'clock Tuesday afternoon. I was met by a Wellesley girl and taken to her home, where her mother, an earlier Wellesley girl, and her father, the brother of one of my classmates, Edith Metcalf, welcomed me with the utmost cordiality. I had hardly eaten my luncheon,—prepared by a Bulgarian boy, an Oberlin student, from whose pleasant and well-to-do home, with parents, tall brother and laughing little sister, a house in the midst of a great flower-garden which was the family pride, he has heard not a syllable since last September and fears it is all death and ashes now,—when Wellesley folk began to call, one at a time, running up to supper. Then I sallied forth on the arm of Mr. Metcalf, who is a trustee, and spent the evening in promenading about an illuminated, festive town. You know how they build a town in the Middle West, just a checkerboard laid out anywhere in the endless prairie, but these straight streets were shaded by long rows of elms and maples and bordered by beautifully kept lawns and flower-gardens, with stately college buildings rising at intervals in the lines of pleasant homes. Japanese lanterns were everywhere, and all the town was out, in all sorts of attire, and all the alumni and alumnae were back with their youngsters, and the Presidential receiving line stood in the plaza before the chapel, and the alumni procession paraded past, headed by two veterans of '64, who bore a banner that said, "Forty-five men in our class; thirty enlisted; fifteen stayed to graduate." Each reunion class, with that honorable exception, tried to be funnier than the rest, but I enjoyed the children most,—sturdy little fellows that would hold up brave banners saying: "When we grow up, we're going to Oberlin, just like Pa." The prize was given to the class that established the Oberlin mission in China, for they made a most picturesque display with all manner of Chinese personages and vehicles. Their babies were trotting mandarins. The next morning Mr. Metcalf showed me the beautiful memorial arch, at the entrance of the campus, for the martyrs of the Boxer massacre. It is like Oberlin that, in addition to the names of their own graduates, they have inscribed the names of their fellows in martyrdom.

Commencement Day was cloudy, with rain while we were all housed for the exercises, and the luncheon later on, but with cool, misty weather for our marching. It's really a physical stunt to take an honorary degree. First you stand around for an hour, all capped and gowned, and meet a lot of strangers. Then you march and march through files of uncapped alumni, over the campus and up the street, hither and thither, like children playing a game. And even when you are finally deposited in your seat on the platform, if you are in the front row, as I was, you have to keep up the proprieties and dignities. I didn't succeed in that at Oberlin, for my marching mate, Dr. Fairchild, was a son of sin and poured a constant stream of nonsense into my left ear, while my right was cocked to catch President King's solemn remarks to the successive candidates for degrees. But I managed to get through my own special part of the show, tho' everything was done with such pomp and ceremony that my knees shook beneath me. When Dr. Wager, the very nice professor of English, who had been cramming on me for a month past, rose and remarked that it was not possible for Oberlin to fail to honor pure literature and that they had an excellent example of such literature combined with distinguished scholarship in a lady (up pops K.L.B. and stands mutely declaring to the audience; "That's me!") who has for twenty-five years been a professor of English literature in a great college for women etc. etc. etc., and when President King, who stood looking as impressed as if he had never heard me mentioned before, opened his august mouth (forth trots K.L.B. till an imperceptible Presidential wink halts her just six feet from the Presence) and addressed me by my full name, assuring me that I was a "discerning scholar" and that my books were of "nation-wide renown" and that my hymn, whose last stanza he recited, expressed, etc. etc. etc., and therefore, by the authority of Oberlin College and of the State of Ohio, he conferred upon me etc. etc. etc., and when I grasped my diploma (which was bogus, as the honorary diplomas hadn't come) I trembled along (it seemed a mile) past him to the two stalwart professors who put on my hood, all crimson and gold, and had almost run back to my chair again, and been applauded so long I had to rise and bow to hush it up,—well, I was glad it was done and over.

I had to speak at the luncheon—they sang the hymn after I finished—, but I didn't mind that half as much. There was some magnificent speaking—not mine—at the luncheon, for Oberlin has a wonderful lot of graduates. It's the most democratic place in the country, I believe, for it gave its chief honors to a negro (the new head of Tuskegee) and a Jew (that splendid Morgenthau), and the Commencement orator was a Cambridge Unitarian! In fact, I am very enthusiastic about my new college.

Everybody was exceedingly kind to me. The Metcalfs were

hospitality itself. One professor took me all about the town in his motor that afternoon, and another took me in his to the train the next morning. There was a Glee Club concert that evening, and people called in all the interstices of the day. In fact, the train was so full of Oberlin people that I was almost smothered with courtesies until we reached Cleveland, at about noon Thursday.

Thanks to your gift and to Jean's energies, I had just the right clothes, social and academical, for the occasion, and I was very appreciative of it all.

Katharine had long hoped that a way might be found to bring outstanding poets to Wellesley to read from their poems and hold informal meetings and discussions. Eminent artists had visited the college from time to time, both musicians and writers. Katharine frequently introduced the guests and then, with a talent which combined the social with the artistic, moved about creating that delightful cohesion of elements that made such events memorable. Among the visitors were Matthew Arnold, Oliver Wendell Holmes, William Sharp (who steadfastly denied, as he met Katharine's keen glance, that he and Fiona Macleod were one and the same), Alice Meynell, Margaret Deland, Julia Ward Howe, Frances Willard, Kate Douglas Wiggin, Booker T. Washington, Emma Eames, and Mme Schumann-Heink.

Her desire was that an established schedule of such visits might be arranged as a yearly addition to the literature program, and through her enthusiasm and the interest and generosity of an alumna, Eunice C. Smith, a series of poets' readings was begun. Old friends came, and new. They stayed often at the Scarab, lingering to enjoy the friendly hospitality, the shop talk, and the serious discussion. When their welcome was a bit outstayed (for Katharine's many responsibilities did not wait upon poets), she telephoned Mrs. Bradford, suggesting innocently that since "Mr. A." knew that he was in Mr. Bradford's neighborhood and had expressed a wish to meet him, perhaps Mrs. Bradford would like to entertain the poet. Responding nobly, Mrs. Bradford would come to the rescue, and "Mr. A." would be carried off for dinner, while Katharine hurried to her desk and work. But when next she saw her accommodating neighbors, Mr. Bradford would look at her sternly and say, "Now be honest! Did he so much as mention my name or say that he wanted to meet me until *you* suggested it?" On one occasion, when Katharine had shared a visitor with the Bradfords, Mr. Bradford made his acknowledgment of the supposed favor very emphatically in verse:

The Poet

A poet visits us. And I
See clearly, when he goes,
The incapacity of my
Staid soul for aught but prose.

His hair was long, his foot was light,
His eyes superbly wild.
Except when forced to be polite,
You knew he never smiled.

His voice had sombre tints of woe,
Gleams of prophetic fire.
His loose tie fluttered to and fro,
Symbolic of desire.

I have no hair, no eyes, no voice,
A poet not worth a damn.
But I confess I quite rejoice
To be the thing I am.

John Masefield's visit was among the most notable. Yeats came, and Robert Frost, Carl Sandburg, John G. Neihardt, Vachel Lindsay, Leonard Bacon, Bliss Carman, Walter de la Mare, Alfred Noyes, George E. Woodberry, and Wilfred Wilson Gibson. There were women poets, too: Lizette Woodworth Reese, Anna Hempstead Branch, Amy Lowell, Leonora Speyer, Florence Converse, Nancy Byrd Turner, and many others. Some of the poets returned to Wellesley more than once, and some came to the Scarab just to renew the friendship with Katharine. Others corresponded with her, seeking her opinions and counsel. Of Masefield, Katharine wrote to a member of her family, "A man whose face is fixed in sorrow, and no wonder, for he is just back from the Dardanelles, where he saw suffering and death, heroism and the victory of spirit over body, on every side. He was with the Red Cross, but was, like the rest, continually under fire. Two close friends sailed out with him, but he left their graves on one of those old Greek isles of melodious name, and is not yet over the wonder of it, that he should be what he was, while they are 'a pulse in the Eternal Mind.' "

Among the poets who came to Wellesley the younger men in particular found sympathy and inspiration in their talks with Katharine. Mr. O'Conor, Mr. Gibson, and Leonard Bacon were especially dear to her. Of Mr. Gibson she wrote to a former student, "He is as true a poet and as beautiful a spirit as I have ever known, and his visit was a wonderful refreshment." Mr. O'Conor lived for a time in or near Boston, and she followed his literary career with loving interest. He wrote to her, "Much of what is good in me is due to your comfort and friendship." For Leonard Bacon she had an especial affectionate regard, not only for his own sake, but for Miss Hazard's.

In the work of the young women poets she found, in general, little evidence of developing maturity. Too many candles were burning at both ends. A hard, brittle adolesence, a deliberate intent to shock, caused her to lay aside their slender volumes in distaste, but here and there a poem or a shining line presaged a future depth of thought. "Youth's visionary hour is brief, at best," she wrote. "One would not see any of its fine gold spent in the small change of cleverness." She was at times reminded of certain of her students who amused themselves by using in her presence modern terms they hoped were daring. They forgot—if indeed they knew—her familiarity with the unexpurgated texts of the fifteenth and sixteenth centuries. She found it difficult to assume a properly shocked expression. There were, however, exceptions among the young women. One was a student and poet of whom she wrote, "Viola White made a shining in the seminar." From "the thin volumes of fantastic jackets and riddling titles, finding still the contortions and distortions of youthful agony, cynicism, derision of the world and of its Maker," she turned in relief to the books her friends Josephine Preston Peabody (Mrs. Lionel Marks), Abbie Farwell Brown, Sara Teasdale, and others sent to her. The work of many of these poets she reviewed for Boston and New York papers.

As a matter of taste Katharine preferred the traditional forms in poetry. In reviewing Edward Thomas' *Harvest of Youth,* she wrote, "This volume does not seek to storm Parnassus by short cuts of eccentricity but follows the path, kissing, like Chaucer's 'litel book,' the footprints of the master." She was in agreement with Gamaliel Bradford who did not "care for the jazz-like innovations in metre nor the showy extravagances which today are taken for sentiment."

Katharine's letters to young poets were carefully written and were full of sound criticism and helpful advice. To one she wrote, "I am greatly interested in all these poems. They are alive, with a certain restless energy flickering through them. They have the human quality of quest—the quest that

Memorial Tablet in the Fenway, Boston

recognizes law and would escape from the difficulties of the way by ascent and not by evasion. I get glimpses through these poems of a brave soul that keeps the vision. I very much appreciate a certain reality and sincerity of expression that strikes up through your verses." She advised all young beginners, "Pour imagination into every word and give every phrase its inevitable form." One poet, startled by first acceptance, wrote hurriedly for advice, and she replied, "No, you don't acknowledge an acceptance. You sit proudly back and wait for your check. Yet remember that the poem is no better than it was before acceptance, and that rejection does not dim the beauty, in reality, of the abashed poem that comes home again. . . . The poem is *it;* tho' editorial favor and checks are nice to have."

Katharine had a special admiration for the work of Thomas S. Jones, Jr. A year before her death he sent her a series of quatrains which she described in a letter to him as "the purest, most heart-encompassing Easter chant that I have known, fresh upon the winds, this many a year." Two of the stanzas touched her deeply:

As quietly as dawns the day's first flush,
As buds unfolding when the warm rains cease,
As stars that gather in the twilight hush,—
So comes the knowledge of Eternal Peace.

Immortal Love is like a shoreless sea,
As boundless as ethereal realms of air;
The Soul doth like an island tranquilly
Rest in Its hallowed beauty unaware.

She said of these lines, "They are the truth of inmost spiritual life as I, even I, have known it." She quoted other lines in an article she was then writing for the *Boston Evening Tran-*

script. In this way she encouraged the young poets, publicly when she could, or privately by letter.

Quotations from her letters to Leonard Bacon are illustrative of her humorous relish of situations as well as of her interest and thoughtful comments: "One of the many pleasures of my visit, just closing, with your Aunt Caroline, has been the hearing of your 'Sophia Trenton,' which she reads with quite remarkable gusto. She read it to me on the second evening after my arrival and last Sunday, when Mr. Waldo was here for dinner and the afternoon, began it again, but was called off by other callers and passed it to me. I read for a little and then gave it over to Mr. Waldo, who read it cautiously, like one skating on thin ice. 'It sounds like Don Juan,' he said, and in the terror of the thought he carefully expurgated as he read, leaving out, for example, that dreadful stanza about Mrs. Percy's brushing her hair in her husband's presence. He was greatly amused by the poem as a whole, but asked if you were not 'telling family secrets.' One or two of your relatives seem a little troubled over it, as if it indicated that you were not happy in your profession. But I don't feel it so at all. Education is, and always has been, mainly a blunder, and the 'teaching' of literature is essentially impossible, of course; but there are more as well as less legitimate approaches to it and I believe you do the cause a service in pointing out its absurdities and evils. Not all Ph. D. research is thrown away, but enough of it is useless, and worse than useless, to make me hope your satire will have a wide circulation."

She wrote to Mr. Bacon of his *Dunbar Tragedy*: "It is clear that you can say anything in the world that you want to say, and say it in the most penetrating and poignant manner. It is quite true, too, that the sister of *your* satire at least is pity. But do you mean to be a satirist forever and ever? If you do, we must all look to our ways! . . . What I can't help hoping is that as the sequence proceeds the satiric element will gradually give place to something more constructive and inspiring. But you must follow your own star, already so bright, and promising to become brighter and brighter."

At a later date she wrote of another of Mr. Bacon's long poems, a letter also dealing with the type of incident she quietly enjoyed:

A Boston University professor was calling on me last Friday afternoon and I made him, to his pretended indignation, read "Quincibald" (what *does* the name mean?) aloud. He insisted, by the way, that the name was satire for Archibald, with a glancing reference to Peter Quince, but I was not satisfied with that. As he read, it irritated him—exasperated him—but he couldn't leave it alone! To be sure, he flung it down after a few pages, but soon caught it up again, reading *passim* with mingled wrath and fascination.

I suspect you like that!

I have read it all three times and parts of it several times more, and I like it better, or, rather, understand and appreciate it more, with every reading. But if you *will* be Dante and swoop into the depths, you are bound to be Dante to the end and find your way up the terraced mountain and on through the crystal spheres to the White Rose whose fragrance does drift down even to Mediocria. In your own parlance, you say so yourself.

Mr. Bradford protests that your metre is not musical, and usually it isn't, but your *mood* isn't musical,—nor your macaw. The metre seems to me to fit the situation.

As Imagism became the rage of the hour and its exponents moved spectacularly across the stage, vigorously led by Amy Lowell, Katharine looked on, interested and somewhat amused. She wrote to a correspondent:

As the Imagists explain themselves, and as the world explains them, they are trying to bring poetry closer to the actual object, to bring the sense perceptions to bear on the visible creation more keenly. It is not a new position. Arnold and Henley both wrote superbly in free verse. Unrhymed verse is no new thing. Always there is the restless attempt to increase methods of expression. . . . The Imagists have done well to call poetry back again to the eyes and ears and away from books. But they have done ill in trying to *confine* poetry to the world of sense, denying the world of spirit. The whole question of Mysticism boils down to the question whether the visible creation is itself the ultimate or a language. Miss Lowell would claim it as ultimate. Emerson is our greatest poet among those who recognize it as the voice of the Spirit.

As for the use of rhyme, she agreed with Arthur Symons, who had said, "To do without rhyme is to do without one of the beauties of poetry."

Amy Lowell (Katharine's associate in the New England Poetry Club, although their pleasant acquaintance never ripened into friendship) did not write poetry with a strong appeal to Katharine's tastes. Yet, with the publication of Miss Lowell's sonnets to Eleanora Duse, Katharine gave her full credit. In a letter to Miss Lowell she wrote, "You may remember how I rejoiced in your closing Duse sonnets where you were using nature as language rather than ultimate, with no less beauty in image but with a new significance and inflooding of spirit."

Katharine agreed with John Masefield that man is "a spiritual being, and the proper work of his mind is to interpret the world according to his higher nature." She knew that "on the uplands, not the lowlands of life shall we find, as humanity has ever found, freedom, freshness, adventure." She felt that American verse had too long concerned itself with man's baser nature, but that a nobler strain would be heard more and more clearly. She herself had written:

"The Splendor Bides Within"

At some far torch of gold
The shining soul was lit
And claims celestial kin
Shadows its house enfold,
But are not one with it.
The splendor bides within.

XXIII

"I Give You Joy"

IN 1909 Katharine had heard Woodrow Wilson, then president of Princeton University, deliver the Phi Beta Kappa address at Harvard. Wilson had won her entire admiration with his words on that day. In the following years she became completely devoted to his ideals and purposes. After his death a dinner was held in honor of his birthday. Katharine was one of the speakers, and as an introduction to her more serious remarks, she described her "first, last and only bet." Referring to the Phi Beta Kappa oration, she said:

His theme was the perennial theme,—how to make the intellectual interest dominant in American college life. He had the vision of a university as a democratic community with the aim of equipping its students, through liberal learning and mental discipline, for leadership in the national life, and he was vigorously and constructively intent on making his vision a reality. The speaker's treatment of his subject was so keen and firm, his language so delightful, that I came home enthusiastic and tried that evening to arouse a sympathetic rapture in a chance caller. He listened with that indulgent masculine amusement so exasperating to womankind and still held the view that our colleges were right enough as they were with athletics and social clubs as their main features. So I naturally grew warmer in my advocacy of an intellectual quality and ethical purpose in college life, until at last, now at white heat, I exclaimed: "I wish we might have a man like that, an original thinker with the courage to put his thought into action, in the White House. I wish this very Woodrow Wilson might be our next president.

And then my caller, with the frankness of an old friend, threw back his head and guffawed loud and long.

"I'll bet you five pounds of Huyler's Best that he won't," he said. "You'll never see Woodrow Wilson president of the United States."

"I take the bet," I responded promptly, running over in my mind how many dollars of a mere professor's salary my rashness would cost me. I took my losing as a matter of course, for I was not aware of the schemes that for three years past Colonel Harvey had been revolving in his head; but from that summer of 1909 I watched the career of the president of Princeton with a personal interest.

Nominated later for the highest political office in the State, Mr. Wilson left Princeton and became Governor of New Jersey. In the summer of 1912 this Governor received the nomination of the Democratic party for President of the United States. On the day when this nomination was flaring from the front pages of the newspapers, I reminded my caller by telephone of our bet. He answered, but not in his former tone of indulgent banter, that there was many a slip twixt the cup and the lip; but as soon as the election count was sure, his youngest child, a small boy of a reproachful countenance, delivered at my door a five-pound box of Huyler's Best.

Upon Wilson Katharine rested all her hope for peace. As time passed she saw clearly what her country must do and used what talents she possessed in service to the cause he led. She could not stand aside while young compatriots, obeying the law of their land, went out perhaps to die.

Requests for poems came at once from the Red Cross, the Y.M.C.A., the Liberty Loans, and many magazines and newspapers. Written against time, and to order, they are not her best poems, but her idealism is apparent in them, as in everything she wrote, and the letters came flooding in from men about to leave, from bereaved families as the casualty lists grew, and from friends and fellow-poets.

The question of pacifism preoccupied her thoughts. Several of her closest friends were publicly avowed pacifists, but their reasoning she could not accept. Writing to one of them of the case of a conscientious objector condemned to a year's imprisonment, she said:

> He has his luxury. There is a law of the land, a land governed by the chosen representatives of the people, and he chose to defy it in the name of his very special conscience. I don't think a year in jail is a very heavy penalty to pay for that defiance. He will enjoy, at least, the sense of virtue.
>
> I'm not exactly ironic about this. The whole thing pulls at my mind when I ought, for example, to be reading final papers. There must be law, mustn't there? Individuals have often thought themselves wiser and their actions better than the law, and some of them were right in thinking so. But isn't that sense of rightness their natural compensation?
>
> I don't feel that this nation goes into this war in a spirit of hate. I don't see that your Pacifists, as an organization, emphasize love. You can't over-emphasize the horrors of war, but the only program before the world today for ending war is to end *this* war by disarming Prussia.
>
> I feel like a concentrated heart-ache going about this queer detail of education with visions of battlefields and cries of bombarded towns always in my ears and soul.

Since the outbreak of war in 1914 Katharine had remained in close touch with English friends, and she had felt more and more strongly that the United States must stand with England in a war which she hoped, as did all Americans, would end war for all time. A poem of an earlier period, a sonnet addressed to England, she later grouped with her war poems, since it was expressive of her feeling during the war years:

America to England

Who would trust England, let him lift his eyes
To Nelson columned o'er Trafalgar Square,
Her hieroglyph of duty, written where
The roar of traffic hushes to the skies;
Or mark, while Paul's vast shadow softly lies
On Gordon's statued sleep, how praise and prayer
Flush through the frank young faces clustering there
To con that kindred rune of sacrifice.
O England, no bland cloud-ship in the blue,
But rough oak plunging on o'er perilous jars
Of reef and ice, our faith will follow you
The more for tempest roar that strains your spars
And splits your canvas, be your helm but true,
Your courses shapen by the eternal stars.

Yet to resort to force was shameful, and Katharine condemned it even while she upheld her country's stand. Hatred of Germany was not part of her attitude toward the world catastrophe. She tracked down and destroyed slander circulating about German friends and colleagues, and she advised the college to continue subscriptions to German periodicals, believing that German scholarship should be given the benefit of the doubt. Through all the war years her point of view was one of protest and pity and of hope that her country could, by joining the allies, bring the war more quickly to an end and take full part in establishing a lasting peace.

During the war Katharine was engaged upon her last volume of prose, *Sigurd*. The book was Sigurd's story and was dedicated to the memory of Katharine Coman. It contained sketches of other Scarab pets,—cats, dogs, and birds who had their day in a haven of kindliness and care. The book had a mixed reception. Several reviewers found it a long-drawn-out rhapsody about a collie, spoiled by the "emotionalism, sponge cake, and fudge of a feminine community." Others had only praise for it. Among the latter was Albert Payson Terhune, whose right to speak on collies was undisputed. He wrote, "She has written a dog biography which merits, to the full, that sadly abused adjective 'great.' The infinitely appealing pen picture of her golden collie is a portrait that must live." His enthusiasm for the book was expressed in print and publicly on every possible occasion, and he immediately made friends with the author. The correspondence thus begun continued over several years, Katharine taking pleasure in reviewing her new friend's famous collie stories. Of *Sigurd* Mr. Terhune wrote to Katharine, "Of course you know in part what you've achieved in 'Sigurd.' But perhaps you don't realize the complete beauty of the book and its hold on every student of the collie. Your book is a masterpiece; in the best sense of that badly abused word. Its pathos is never bathos. Its sentiment is never sentimentality. It is a gem. I have made some slight study of the collie in the course of forty odd years and at every angle and every facet, your delineation is flawless."

It had been a pleasure to Katharine to write the book, reviving as it did, memories of the day when she and Katharine Coman had brought Sigurd home from Cedar Hill in 1903. She was glad that the majority of the critics felt that her sense of humour had steered her clear of sentimentality. Collie owners wrote to her from all over the country, thanking her for the book, and Mr. Terhune named his famous "Sunnybank Sigurd" for Katharine's dog. Later, when she had sent him a picture of herself with Hamlet, her second collie friend, he wrote her a letter that rewarded all her effort with her strange, nervous companion: "He is a beauty. And his expression is not that of a stricken or perpetually frightened dog. You have cured him;—and not one such case in four is cured. He will never be aggressive; but he is no longer cowed. If ever you must leave him, permanently, send him on to wait for you, rather than leave him in charge of outsiders. A very little ill treatment would revive all his olden chronic fright."

In prose and in poetry Katharine had learned well the hard lessons of authorship. She had found the chief difficulties to be four. First, and greatest, was the sense of the need to write, accompanied by the consciousness that too soon "all our little strength is done." Hurrying, crowded days continually postponed the poems that waited to be written in solitude and peace. She put second the lack of understanding (with which she, herself, happily had to contend very little), the point of view which seemed to say, "Why should it be any work to write?" Emerson, folding his arms beside the brook, may have presented a picture of idleness, but every aster that he carried home was "loaded with a thought." Third was the struggle between the artistic conscience and the "inner consciences," the patriotic, the social, and the domestic. What author would not wish to "blazon on the outside of his study door Ben Jonson's bluff inhospitality:

> *I will not have Good Fortune, or God's Blessing,*
> *Let in, while I am busy."*

Fourth, and most wearing of all, was the actual "poetic wrestling" and the resulting irritation, like "lightning playing on the edges of one's temper."

The "inner consciences" often prevailed in Katharine's life as she lent her energies to various projects and to the needs of the college. Always buoyed up by the sense that she was "getting ready to achieve," she went on with the "endless picture puzzle of life."

In October, 1919, she was "solemnly waited on by a delegation of four to request that I let my phiz be painted." The artist was to be the distinguished marine painter, Charles H. Woodbury. Neither artist nor subject was entirely satisfied as the work progressed through some forty sittings. But in the time thus spent a fine friendship developed, and Katharine did not begrudge the many hours lost from her work.

Wellesley now owns another portrait, the one used in this book, which was painted by an artist whose work is primarily in portraiture. Copied from photographs after Katharine's death, the painting captures with extraordinary success Katharine's characteristic charm and the bright look with which she welcomed a friend to her study. From this picture those who did not know her may apprehend something of the personality of the woman who was called the "center of Wellesley's love and loyalty."

Katharine had long looked forward to 1920 as her year of retirement, but pension regulations were changed, which made it necessary that she continue to teach for another five years. It was a severe blow to her plans for the future, and also a matter of some anxiety, for there had been warnings of a decline in health and strength. Miss Pendleton found it possible to lighten her schedule, reducing her class program to four hours and relieving her of all other college responsibilities.

June, 1920, was a milestone for Katharine. She cleared out her college desk for Miss Sherwood, who took over the chairmanship of the department. The "Eighties" returned for their fortieth reunion, and the Scarab kept open house. Katharine attended her last Academic Council. The summer quiet enveloped the Scarab. Of course, work still lay waiting on the desk at home. Already the committee work for Wellesley's semicentennial to be held in 1925 had begun. But there was a pleasant vacation trip with Miss Hazard, this time to Cape Cod and Falmouth. With thoughts of a more leisurely winter, Katharine was at last able to look forward to the symphony concerts on Friday afternoons. In Europe music had meant much to her, and she had heard great orchestras and famous artists. But in her work-a-day life in Wellesley there was little time for anything beyond the familiar routine. Her relatives came and went in Wellesley, and Katharine could now enjoy old friends without the pressure of scheduled tasks that could not wait.

She had made a small collection of her war poems, adding a few older poems from the earlier volume *America the Beautiful*, now out of print, and some new poems. This collection was published under the title *The Retinue* in 1918. Poetry was now Katharine's first occupation, although she was still reviewing, editing, writing articles, and contributing to the furthering of the League of Nations. Quoting Protagoras, she wrote in an article for the *Boston Evening Transcript*, "The life of man in every part has need of harmony and rhythm. At last she could satisfy that need, which for her was chiefly the creation of harmony and rhythm.

In Katharine's life there now existed a tranquility in which her devoted love for Miss Coman could find expression. She wrote a corona of sonnets, the most deeply felt of all her poems. In a foreword to Katharine's *Selected Poems*, published posthumously, Mrs. Guild wrote, "A Corona, we are told is a series of seven sonnets, bound together in an Italian fashion, by which the first line of each sonnet repeats the last of the one preceding, and the last line of the last sonnet repeats the first line of the first." Katharine had seen but one example in English poetry of the corona, in Donne's series of "Holy Sonnets." She wrote seven groups of seven sonnets. The closing line of the series repeated the opening and closing lines of the first corona: "I give you joy, my Dearest.

Death is done." Joy is the mounting emotion of the entire corona. The word occurs in every one of the forty-seven sonnets. Using phrases from Katharine Coman's notes to her and words of Christ quoted by Miss Coman, gathering all her poignant memories of their long years of service to the college and to their larger allegiances, Katharine wove a remarkable series of sonnets, which stands alone as a memorial written by a woman to a woman.

After the opening section of rejoicing in the triumphant victory of her friend over pain and death, the thought turns back to the earliest days of Miss Coman's childhood, to the home life and loves, a complete admission of Katharine's own sense of personal grief and loss, memories of their life together, the hope, and then the doubt, of personal immortality, and the search for and avowal of a "faltering faith." The sonnets culminate in an effort to follow the admonition to "hold fast the Life Eternal," with the repetition at the end, "I give you joy."

These sonnets are now little known, since the volumes in which they appeared are out of print. As a whole they express a universal emotion. They rise to an aspiration of faith and hope, and to a selfless joy for the spirit freed of mortality. Many examples might be quoted here to illustrate the poetic achievement. The third sonnet of the seventh corona is especially felicitous in its expression of a common but always overwhelming experience:

Have I not sometimes felt your presence nigh?
You said: "I will not leave you comfortless,"
And oft half conscious of a swift impress
Upon my spirit, lights that clarify
A problem, calm on storm, ever I try
To hold my listening heart in readiness
For joy of your impalpable caress,
Wisdom of your inaudible reply.

Oh, still shed blessing on me from those wings
Of whose soft tarriance I would be aware,
Light intimations, fleet evanishings,
Speech finer than all syllables, a rare
Shining within my soul, a thrill intense
That breaketh not Death's law of reticence.

The sonnet sequence was unique in poetry, for no series of poems had ever been written celebrating the friendship of women—not necessarily "a new type of friendship," as Jane Addams called it in a letter to Katharine, but a relationship developing naturally in the community life of a woman's college. The spiritual and intellectual companionship of women of like mind and taste fostered lifelong devotion and loyalty not unlike the friendships of men. Katharine understood in herself, and recognized in the lives of others, the nobility and dignity of such attachments. The corona was her tribute to a deep and lasting friendship.

When the sonnets were completed, Katharine put with them other poems written about her friend. She called the collection *Yellow Clover.* It was published in 1922 and was her Easter gift to her friends. Those who read the poems found their own expression of love and longing. Katharine had not desired wide recognition for this particular book, but it did not escape the attention of the critics, who found in it substantiation for the belief that there was no truer voice among American poets of the twenties.

Although Katharine continued to write in the few remaining years, *Yellow Clover* was the climax of her poetic aspirations. She had realized her deepest desire—to memorialize the dearest companion of her life. Gladdened by loving and understanding letters, she took up once more the daily tasks and the creative work which was to bring her satisfaction and a quiet contentment.

XXIV

Retirement

As the last decade of Katharine's life began, she copied into her journal Chesterton's lines:

Lo! I am come to autumn
Where all the leaves are gold.

She agreed with Louise Imogen Guiney, who felt that "quotations . . . from the great old authors are an act of filial reverence . . . and a blessing." A quotation borne in mind through a sad or difficult day was an inspiration, and in a day of gladness or accomplishment an added joy. In moments of grief she had sometimes recalled the words of a poet who said,

And grief, that cannot reckon with a mystery,
Is comforted by trifles.

So she turned the small matters of each day into more than trifles and made them all a part of life's adventure: the neighborhood events, the day's mail, the walks with Mrs. Reddell and Hamlet in the woods, the aurora borealis, the spring bulbs, the battle with gray squirrels at the window boxes. Her mail brought many lives into touch with her own, for still the letters came, from friends and strangers, from country folk, lonely folk, travel acquaintances, a Jesuit priest, poets, dog owners, the newly bereaved, those who agreed or disagreed with her politics when her opinions were revealed in interviews. Although there were days when she called the letters "no better than hydra-heads," yet she answered them, sometimes forty or more in a day. They were all a part of life's richness, and each received its acknowledgment until finally, to her family's great relief, she stopped replying to requests for autographs unless a stamped and addressed envelope was enclosed. This was the only instance when she withheld anything she could give.

June, 1925, came, and with it the last seminar, the last commencement, Wellesley's Semicentennial and Katharine's retirement. Of the final seminar, Gamaliel Bradford wrote: "There was something poetic about the atmosphere—and I think we all felt it. It is more than thirty years now since I first went to one of the seminars—and it seems like a good deal of a break to think that I shall not go any more. For Miss Bates it must be a break, indeed, and it would be hard to reckon all that she has given in all those years of inspiration and sympathy."

Katharine had many parts to play, many last appointments to meet and last celebrations to attend, all pervaded by the atmosphere of gaiety and underlying sadness typical of every June on the campus. The farewell seminar dinner, the department dinner, the Phi Beta Kappa banquet, and the Phi Sigma breakfast were held. At the impressive commencement exercises Wellesley conferred upon her the degree of Doctor of Laws, her third honorary degree.

Not all the ties were broken by retirement. Katharine was still busy with committee work in connection with the fund-raising which was a part of the fiftieth celebration. At the request of the *Boston Transcript* she wrote an account of the proceedings and a brief history of Wellesley's proud half-century, the founding, the developments and the accomplishments.

Once more the Scarab kept open house; once more the class of 1880 gathered about their president, to whom they presented a great laurel wreath. Caroline Hazard, who had walked near Katharine in the academic procession and had also received an honorary degree, made her farewell call. Slowly the tide of alumnae ebbed. The campus and the Scarab were quiet again. Katharine confessed that she was tired at the end of forty-five years of teaching but added that she would be ashamed if she were not.

In the year following her retirement she put together the last volume of verse to be published in her lifetime, *The Pilgrim Ship*. Inscribed to Caroline Hazard, it contained the poems of the Egyptian and Palestine months, her Christmas poems, a play, "The Healing of Tobit," and fourteen lyrics grouped under the title "Reveries." She was thinking now of giving up some of her other literary work. She wrote to Arthur, "I want my time to gather my patriotic poems into a volume. Then there may be one volume of the rest, if I live so long and if the patience of the young critics, for whom I am a back number, holds out. I expect vials of scorn will be poured on 'The Pilgrim Ship.' " That expectation, however, was not realized. The reviews were favorable and showed a careful reading of the poems and an appreciation of their content. Mr. Bradford, writing in the *Transcript*, expressed the general admiration and acclaim:

What charms me in Miss Bates's latest volume of verse is its restfulness. With all its varied merits, the poetry of today, for the most part, gives a sense of disquiet. . . . There is . . . a vague and endless questioning, a constant, undisciplined portrayal of varied agitations of the spirit. . . . Miss Bates has her questions also, and she would be the last to deny it. She is well aware of the questions that cannot be answered, of the tumults that cannot be stilled. Yet through it all is that sense of restfulness, of long acquaintance with those regions in which the spirit finds, or at least for centuries has found, its peace. . . .

In these songs of Palestine Pilgrimage is the element that appears in all Miss Bates's work, the sense and instinct of drama, and this is in no way incompatible with the impression of restfulness, for busy, fruitful action does not disquiet the spirit half so much as a tormented external repose. This suggestion of drama, of the possibilities of directed movement, and the presence of purpose in human affairs, informs not only the actual plays, like the charming "Tobit," but even the briefer poems and lyrics. . . . It is easy to see how much Miss Bates has always been influenced by the dramatists whom she loves, by that great, perplexing, enthralling Shakespeare, and, especially in such pieces as "Tobit," by the medieval religious dramas about which she wrote so admirably long ago. . . .

[Another] element of these poems is the strong Christian influence, not in doctrinal assertion of orthodox theory, but in the intense and constant feeling of what the Christian tradition means, or has meant, in the world. This Christian influence of course deeply pervades the book under discussion, since it deals with the external scenes of Jesus's earthly manifestation. . . . There is no preaching in these verses, any more than there is preaching in "America the Beautiful." There is no emphasis on creed, perhaps no intimation of doctrinal belief in any. There is simply the constant realization that the best that humanity has done, perhaps the best it can do, is bound up with that white vision which descended upon Palestine nearly twenty centuries ago. And rich resources of melody and musical stimulus, varied grace of verbal inspiration are used to make that realization as vivid and compelling to the reader as it is to the poet.

Slowly Katharine's life became more circumscribed. It was not easy now for her to walk. But her ever-generous friend, Miss Hazard, gave her an endowed car. With all expenses paid and a chauffeur in charge, an undreamed-of luxury and pleasure came into Katharine's life. It was "like having wings."

Not the least of her joys in it was the pleasure it brought to her sister. It became a familiar sight in the village to see Katharine and Jeannie going about their errands in comfort. They shared with others the refreshment and interest of drives into the surrounding country. The car had its own guest book, and the name of at least one guest was inscribed in it whenever the car was on the road. After Katharine's death the guest book went to Miss Hazard that she might know how far her thoughtfulness had extended and how many had shared her kindness.

On the eve of her sixty-seventh birthday Katharine wrote to a niece: "I expect to be, three hours later, sixty-seven years old, and tomorrow I shall read from the Covenanter's version of the Psalms: 'The days of my years are seventy years of them, or with much strength eighty years they may go, but a weary wrastle all the time of it. In a gliff it goes by, and we flichter hame.' " In a letter the following spring she wrote: "I am thriving, if not like a green bay tree, at least like a pinky-green old oak that is putting on its spring mood with dignified deliberation."

Now every day had a "grace upon it." Life was more leisurely, more casual, more intimate. Hamlet, after ten happy years, was gone. But the family had a pet, a dignified green parrot, a "gay old bird" who was named Polonius "for his musty scraps of wisdom and wit." After his morning toast and coffee Polly was placed in the lower branches of a tree, while Katharine and Jeannie strolled over the small property. After a visit to the Scarab, George E. Woodberry wrote: "The color and attitude of Polonius made the deepest sensational dint on my eyes,—he reminded me of Trajan's column, and seemed a figure fit to cap it! I wonder why he seemed so high majestic,—and what a color!"

Mrs. Reddell made the house a retreat of rest and charm. Mrs. Guild, now living close by, came through the wide south door every evening for dinner and an hour in the study. To Katharine her home and her small plot of ground were dearer than ever. All she asked was "to enjoy what is mine—and with unweakened mind an old age not uncomely or deprived of poetry."

The importunate world still came to her door, and in spite of good resolutions she could not refuse its requests—or its honors. The New England Poetry Club gave her its annual award of the "Golden Rose." To her diary she confided modestly that the award was made "just out of kindliness." It was presented by Foster Damon, and a few of her poems were read by Robert Hillyer, one of the younger poets whose work she admired. The National Hymn Society gave a luncheon in Boston in her honor and made her an honorary member. She assumed the general editorship of a series of children's books to be published by the American branch of Oxford University Press. She assisted Lionel S. Marks in gathering Mrs. Marks's poems for publication, and she wrote the foreword to the collection. As Josephine Preston Peabody, Mrs. Marks had been for a time a member of Wellesley's English Literature department. Katharine had watched the unfolding of her lyrical and dramatic powers and had recognized with keenest pleasure a poet whose aspiration and ideals were much like her own.

A new edition of *Sigurd* came out with a foreword by Albert Payson Terhune. The *Pilgrim Ship* went into its second thousand copies. The *Boston Herald* requested that she write occasional articles, and a national magazine asked the privilege of seeing every poem before it was sent to any other editorial office. There were still many requests for articles on literary subjects which were of special interest to her. Although to her family it seemed that she worked as hard as ever, nevertheless her retirement had eased the strain, and she was able to choose her tasks. She wrote that her days and nights were the most restful of her life. She continued to review new books.

How could she refuse, when the books were by Leonard Bacon, Robert Bridges, Norreys O'Conor, Abbie Farwell Brown, Marion Pelton Guild, Sara Teasdale, Caroline Hazard, and Louise Imogen Guiney?

One review she wrote with reluctance and under pressure. Amy Lowell's *John Keats* was out, and Miss Lowell requested through Allan Nevins of the *New York Sun* that Miss Bates review it for that paper. Katharine protested that her period was the sixteenth century, and suggested a nineteenth-century specialist instead, but finally yielded to insistent requests. Her journal reveals that she never worked harder on any review than on this two-volume work, which was "dashing and brilliant" but not to her "simpatico." To her infinite distress, the review was cut, meanings were altered, and the literary quality destroyed. Miss Lowell wrote to her ruefully that she had brought this least sympathetic review down upon her own head, but that she took it as a compliment that Katharine had taken the trouble to read the books and write upon them. Katharine was sincerely grieved by the episode and regretted that integrity had demanded that she give something less than praise to certain aspects of the work. The incident ended in a generous and understanding telephone call from Miss Lowell which did much to alleviate Katharine's distress.

Although the reviewing was tiring and exacting work she continued it for some time. The very general feeling among her correspondents, lovingly expressed by Sara Teasdale, seemed to place an obligation upon her:

> Another of those keen and gentle reviews of yours has just been read. The impulse to thank you for writing them has become too strong to resist. What you say always covers so much more than the book under consideration that it seems to get at the very spirit of poetry. It opens a door onto the great sunlit

field of literature as a whole, and to point out to the writer of the minute the eternal horizon toward which he may travel. In your review of Miss ——'s book you reached its special malady of the spirit (and that of so many other writers of verse today) so gently and conclusively that she herself must be very grateful to you. How much tact must be added to wisdom to do that, and how much generosity. Mr. Filsinger [her husband] wants me to give his thanks with mine to a poet who is willing to give herself now and then to the writing of criticism that builds up poetry. May it not keep us from having more sonnets like, "I give you joy, my Dearest" or lyrics like the one beginning "If the Celestial Body, ethereal, mystic, remembers—"

A summer of serious illness brought grave anxiety to Katharine's family and friends. But with the arrival of cooler weather she was better than she had expected to be again and recorded "the normal zest for life once more." Mrs. Guild's visit at the end of each day closed her various labors in an atmosphere of quiet, loving companionship. If she had written a poem it was read and discussed, and her friend's criticism was usually accepted. The radio Arthur had presented often provided concerts. Katharine could now have the music she loved and also, to her amusement, football games, prize fights, and political speeches. There were two little grandnieces now living in Wellesley who often dropped in for a game of dominoes with "Aunt Katharine" or a call in "Aunt Jeannie's" room, where they admired the delicate painting on the greeting cards and told school and family anecdotes to a most appreciative audience. And Mrs. Reddell kept a "quiet pulse of order and neatness beating in the Scarab."

XXV

"Dream and Deed"

THE LAST COLLECTION of verse, which Katharine had long been planning, was called *America the Dream.* She dedicated the book to her brother Arthur and chose significant words for the title page: "Where there is no vision, the people perish." The work upon this volume, which was published posthumously, was completed in the last year of her life. Again she included older poems, but the book contained much new work as well, notably lyrics and ballads about the early discoverers and colonists. The preface to this section was a lyric in which she combined a nostalgic yearning for England and the seventeenth-century longing for new lands:

Farewell to England

No more to sleep under the fragrant thatch
Of the grey stone cottage where throstles nest,
For ever a hand would lift the latch
And a wind would whisper out of the west.
Over the vast of lonely sea
To a savage shore without spire or bell!
Ah, it's bewildered our hearts will be!
England, farewell, farewell!

No more to be heaping the harvest wains
In the wise old fields with their golden drift.

"Dream and Deed"

Like shadows we pass from the hawthorn lanes.
The tide is calling; the anchors lift.
Longing shall last while ivy is green;
Home is here wheresoever we dwell.
Glimmering shores no more to be seen,
England, England, farewell!

Another series of poems in *America the Dream* dealt with a group she called "The Forgotten." This section was prefaced by a quotation from Sir Thomas Browne: "Who knows whether the best of men be known, or whether there be not more remarkable persons forgot, than any that stand remembered in the known account of time."

Looking back over the literary output of her career, Katharine found that almost all of her original writings had gone out of print. She felt that there might still be a public for her patriotic poems and for work which she thought of collecting under the title *Dance of the Firelight.* She projected other books to extend through 1932, *The Pope's Ruby, Sparks of Divinity,* and *The Case of Edward Arden.* The last of these was to deal with Shakespeare's uncle, whose little-known career had aroused her imagination. Of these books only the titles had been recorded. She had put some notes together for the book on Arden but had not begun to write. She had planned but later abandoned a travel book on Egypt and Palestine and an Egyptian novel, of which she wrote several chapters. Her editions of the classics were still in print and were widely used. "America the Beautiful" continued to grow in popularity.

Katharine, who had observed the changing poetic fashions of her own day, had no illusions about the eventual fate of her own poetry. Although she counted herself a "back number" at the end of her life, some of her friends prophesied future recognition. Mr. Bradford wrote that "she looked at life and art from the larger, eternal angle, which the too close vision of the day is apt to miss." And Professor Palmer, writing to Mrs. Guild, expressed the opinion that "as soon as the fashions of the day pass her work will hold an assured place among the large things of American poetry."

Although Katharine experienced some of the weaknesses of age, she was only in her late sixties, not old as age is counted today. Of her brothers and sister only Sam had gone. Now separations did not hurt as they once had. She had written for her Eighties, "Death's neighbor tread has lost its threat." The way without old friends would not be long. She came to a mood of quiet acceptance and expectation. In her diary she wrote Emerson's words, "The secret of Heaven is kept from age to age. No imprudent, no sociable angel ever dropt an early syllable to answer the longings of saints, the fears of mortals." But of this hard circumstance, against which she had so often rebelled, she now often said "what matter" and "never mind." She wrote to a cousin of her doctors' order that she must avoid exertion and excitement: "I must be a pious oyster, but I like my orders, for they give me a complete excuse for not speaking in public nor attending luncheons and dinners of these innumerable organizations that eat and talk in hotels and club houses."

Yet, in spite of illness and, at times, great physical discomfort, Katharine felt with Sir Thomas Browne that "the long habit of living indisposeth us for dying." And so, no matter how wearing the night had been, she still looked from her window each morning with joyous expectation in what the day might bring and found "the forsythia brightening" or the "sky warm and blue and beautiful." Of the larger prospect she kept the belief that, in spite of manifold discouragements, the world would yet "mount for Love." Like Emerson, she thought nobly of humanity.

In the spring of 1928 Jeannie became ill and died at the

Scarab. Katharine and Mrs. Reddell were alone at last, and the house was now "too still." She kept to her familiar ways as much as possible and drove to Boston or to Peace Dale, where "a kindly Heaven dropped rain so that I could cover a wrong waist with a right coat." Friends continued to visit her, and each day brought fresh interests. The oldest grandniece became a Wellesley freshman; a new collie puppy came to the Scarab; she celebrated her birthday in Falmouth with Hattie Gifford. But she wrote in her literary record, "Am asked to edit Sylvester Baxter's poems by his executors, but must regretfully decline. I am sorry not to oblige an old friend gone away, but he will understand. I am invited to speak for Poetry at the Abbott Centennial next June,—but life is too uncertain." There was still time for a poem or two, and she wrote "Courage," in part a last word to her classmates, whose president *in absentia* she would always be. She asked Mrs. Guild to send a copy to each Eighty.

At last a day came when Katharine sent for her car and asked to be driven slowly about the campus. It was March and the first touch of spring was in the air. There was a slow stirring of life under the leaf mold, a hint of softening in the pattern of branches against the sky, a warmer light in the sun upon Waban. The great new buildings of the college faded from her sight until there remained only College Hall, the listening woodland, the quiet meadow, and the footpaths where long ago friends walked together in young companionship.

She did not go out or come downstairs again. Infinitely distressed that at last her door must be closed to friends, she spent her last weeks in "Bohemia," reading eagerly the newspaper accounts of the Byrd expedition to the South Pole and writing broken lines of a sonnet to its leader.

Occasionally she mentioned a perplexing dream which had recurred all her life. A small gnomelike figure stood in a corner of her room, his face turned persistently from her as he bent to saw a log of wood. It seemed to her in the dream that at the instant of the log's falling he would turn to look fully at her, when she would see at last the expression on the hidden face. In that moment, she would "perceive it all, the whence, the whither and the why of this that we call life."

She was happy in the companionship of her family. Her brother came from Portland to oversee the practical details of her household and to tease her about her checkbook, which it was his habit to inspect with her from time to time. Sam's son, Dr. William Bates, in whom she felt great pride, came when his busy life permitted. Her nieces often visited her. Their children, now numbering six, were very dear to her. She asked many questions about them and found a special interest in each one. In Philadelphia a grandniece, her namesake, carried on her name, and a grandnephew bore her father's name, William. Mrs. Guild, Mrs. Reddell, and two nurses were with her constantly. She spoke of her joy in the love of those about her, but said she felt like "a dullard kept after school." She asked to hear the Psalms and prayers she had loved for so long. Early on the morning of March 28, 1929, as Mrs. Guild was reading Whittier's "At Last" in her low, familiar voice, Katharine's quiet breathing gently ceased.

Looking from a window at the Scarab a little later, a member of the family saw a movement of color against the cloudless spring sky. Slowly the flag on Tower Court fluttered down and then rose to half-staff. The college had learned of its loss. As the news spread, a feeling almost of desolation gripped those to whom Katharine had meant so much. To others, in the words of her friend Miss Scudder, "Earth became a lonelier and a colder place when her warmth and valor were withdrawn." But the lessons she had taught of the search for Truth, of beauty, of idealism, of unselfish love, were not forgotten with her going.

To the family plot at Falmouth Katharine's ashes came home to rest. While writing out directions for her cremation, she had said, "I like to think how light they'll be." She chose her own inscription to be added to those cut in the plain shaft above the graves of her parents and sister, "I will sing unto the Lord a new song." But those who loved her keep in memory another epitaph, her own words:

We are our own longing, thus
Let Love remember us.

No one who wrote or spoke publicly of Katharine Lee Bates after her death better described her and her work than Leonard Bacon, who gave a memorial address in Boston at the dedication of a tablet to her memory. He said in part:

Her own poetry has spoken for itself [today] and with a better voice than mine. It is distinguished for grace elegance and poignancy. Though much of it is lyrically tragic she could not take great things morosely. That labored intellectual gloom which has too often turned the right-minded away from portentous poets wallowing in artificial melancholy was not and could not be hers. She knew like Montaigne before her that: "The most evident token and apparant signe of true wisdome is a constant and unconstrained rejoycing, whose estate is like unto all things above the Moone, that is, ever clear, alwaies bright." And a sincere simplicity of spirit went always joyfully with delicacy, humor and gentleness.

As the great old proverb goes, We have what we have lost. In as lubric and adulterate an age as John Dryden's own, she shaped without violence innumerable lives into grace and kindliness. What we do today is largely unnecessary. For the fire of enlightenment, whose minister she was, is not quenched by many waters. The witnesses to the continuity of such an influence are numberless and they increase. Perhaps we only testify to our own intelligence when we pay our tribute to vital and charming personality that does not perish.

After the acceptance of loss, the first thought of those who had loved her was, How may we honor her memory? Wellesley College held a memorial service in the chapel at which Miss Scudder made the principal address. Miss Hazard, to whom the news had come in California, endowed a chair of English literature in her name at Wellesley and commissioned Mr. Albert Herter to paint murals illustrating "America the Beautiful" for the Blue Lounge at Green Hall. Eunice C. Smith, of the class of 1898, who had already brought many poets to Wellesley, established a fund in Katharine's name for permanent poetry readings. The portrait painted by Mary Cotheal Burgess of Philadelphia was given to the college. A former student, Mrs. Frank T. Gorman, presented the Falmouth Free Library with a collection of Katharine's books and asked J. Sanger Atwill of Lynn to make a special case for them. The New York Federation of Women's Clubs announced that in May following her death a memorial tree would be set out on Riverside Drive. Money was raised by public subscription for a memorial tablet in Boston. Designed by the sculptor John Francis Paramino, the bronze tablet, set in a plain granite stone, bears her name, the dates of her birth and death, and an inscription composed by Caroline Hazard and Gamaliel Bradford: "Scholar Patriot Poet who gave enduring speech to the love of Americans for America." Below are the words of the first stanza of "America the Beautiful." A design of yellow clover and laurel leaves forms the border of the tablet. It stands near a road and footpath in the Fenway in Boston, sheltered by two gnarled and venerable birches. The Museum of Fine Arts may be seen in the distance. Katharine would have approved the location.

In addition to *America the Dream*, a new edition of *From*

Gretna Green to Land's End was published after Katharine's death. In place of the projected volume, *Dance of the Firelight*, Mrs. Guild and Earl Marlatt of the faculty of the Boston University School of Theology compiled a selection of those poems which they felt she would most care to have included. This volume was published under the title *Selected Poems* with a foreword written by Mrs. Guild.

Mindful of an agreement made some time before with Katharine, Mr. Bradford wrote the obituary for the Wellesley newspaper, *The Townsman*. Because it is an affectionate and sincere tribute from one who knew her well, it is included here:

The death of Katharine Lee Bates means the passing away of one of the most notable citizens of Wellesley, one of the most important figures connected with Wellesley College, and much more than that, a considerable author and creative influence in the whole of American life. Though not born in Wellesley, Miss Bates may be regarded as having always identified herself most deeply and affectionately with the life of our town.

Everyone who writes verse with such enthusiasm as Miss Bates gave to it would prefer to be looked upon first of all as a poet, but few have a better claim to be so regarded than she. She was a poet in spirit as well as in practice, and the poetical, the imaginative attitude entered into every phase and aspect of her life. It was not only that she wrote verses, from the time she was a child until her old age. The touch of prophetic inspiration, the larger, emotional, ideal interpretation of life entered into all her interests and all her practical concerns. Whether it was art, or nature, or social life, or politics, she saw all of them in the broader, loftier, more enduring light of spiritual value. And at the same time, she did this always with the saving touch of humor. She would not take even idealism too seriously, with the portentous solemnity that so often turns it into pedantry. When creeds and theories and arguments grew too heavy and too strained, she had always ready the delicate touch of light laughter to turn acrimony into grace.

She was the poet in her scholarship. She was trained in the best traditions of thoroughness and exactitude. She allowed herself no carelessness, no slip-shod methods, no laxity. Work must be done patiently and well. But it was only worth doing because there was imagination and the ideal behind it. No amount of drudgery could deter this indefatigable worker, but the drudgery was mere dust and ashes, unless it was inspired by the god of sunlight and joy.

So she was the poet in her teaching. You could not elude her with superficial methods. She knew those who were workers and just how to make them work. She knew how to demand exhaustive research and knew how to inspire the dullest and also the idlest with the ambition to do it. But here again it was not the mere work that counted. It was first of all the love of lovely things that she sought to give you and did give you, because it was the spirit and the inspiration of her own life.

And she was perhaps supremely the poet in friendship. The highest reach of that ideal devotion is only known and appreciated by those who saw something of it in its most chosen working, but the same poetic depth and richness were in due measure available and obtainable for all her friends at any time. There was the gracious play of gayety and merriment, the light and easy gift of turning daily difficulties and social accidents into the pleasant passage of a summer jest. But always under this was the higher imaginative sympathy, the power of understanding other lives and other loves, of entering into them, of drawing confidence and treasuring it and returning it in ample measure, which brought to Miss Bates the broadest friendship, from her old pupils, from her literary associates, from all those who had to deal with her in any human relation and who were sure that they could count upon her to the last for wise counsel and unfailing loyal support.

And finally this poet wrote "America the Beautiful." Many years ago it was said, "Let me make the songs of a country, I care not who makes its laws." To have put the expression of the highest and deepest patriotism into the mouths of a hundred million Americans is a monument so noble and so enduring that it seems as if no poet could possibly ask or expect anything more complete.

A long, fruitful, and happy life had ended. No final estimate can be made of that life; it continues in many lives, often unrecognized and far-reaching. It is an emanation lingering from the ideals of one who had her being in love and had joy in that love—one who left, expressed in her own fashion, a last acknowledgment before she turned to meet the "Life Eternal":

The Debt

Because the years are few, I must be glad;
Because the silence is so near, I sing;
'Twere ill to quit an inn where I have had
Such bounteous fare nor pay my reckoning.
I would not, from some gleaming parapet
Of Sirius or Vega, bend my gaze
On a remembered sparkle and regret
That from it thanklessly I went my ways
Up through the starry colonnades nor found
Violets in any Paradise more blue
Than those that blossomed on my own waste ground
Nor vespers sweeter than the robins knew.

Though earth be but an outpost of delight,
Heaven's wild frontier by tragedy beset,
Only a Shakespeare may her gifts requite,
Only a happy Raphael pay his debt.

Yet I, to whom, even as to these, are given
Cascading foam, emblazoned butterflies,
The moon's pearl chariot through the massed clouds driven
And the divinity of loving eyes,
Would make my peace now with mine hostess Earth,
Give and take pardon for all brief annoy,
And toss her, far beneath my lodging's worth,
Poor that I am, a coin of golden joy.

Works by Katharine Lee Bates

(The following list repeats an informal memorandum made by Katharine Lee Bates. The only exceptions, included here, are *English Drama, A Working Basis*, which is widely used today and is considered of great importance, and posthumous publications.)

POETRY

The College Beautiful and Other Poems. Boston, H. O. Houghton, 1887.

Relishes of Rhyme (pseud. "James Lincoln"). Boston, Richard G. Badger, 1903.

America the Beautiful and Other Poems. New York, Thomas Y. Crowell Company, 1911.

The Retinue and Other Poems. New York, E. P. Dutton and Company, 1918.

Yellow Clover, A Book of Remembrance. New York, E. P. Dutton and Company, 1922.

The Pilgrim Ship. New York, The Woman's Press, 1926.

America the Dream. New York, Thomas Y. Crowell Company, 1930 (published posthumously).

Selected Poems. Boston, Houghton Mifflin Company, 1930 (published posthumously).

PROSE

The English Religious Drama. New York, Macmillan and Company, 1893.

American Literature. New York, The Macmillan Company, 1897 (school edition, 1908).

Spanish Highways and Byways. New York, The Macmillan Company, 1900.

From Gretna Green to Land's End. New York, Thomas Y. Crowell and Company, 1907.

Sigurd our Golden Collie and Other Comrades of the Road. New York, E. P. Dutton and Company, 1919.

TRANSLATION

Becquer, Gustavo Adolfo. *Romantic Legends of Spain* (with Cornelia Frances Bates). New York, Thomas Y. Crowell and Company, 1909.

POETRY FOR CHILDREN

Sunshine and Other Verses. Printed by the Wellesley Alumnae, 1890.

The Story of Chaucer's Canterbury Pilgrims. New York, Rand, McNally and Company, 1909.

Fairy Gold. New York, E. P. Dutton and Company, 1916.

Little Robin Stay-Behind and Other Plays in Verse for Children. New York, The Woman's Press, 1924.

PROSE FOR CHILDREN

Rose and Thorn. Boston, The Congregational Sunday-School and Publishing Society, 1889.

Hermit Island. Boston, D. Lothrop Company, 1890.

In Sunny Spain with Pilarica and Rafael. New York, E. P. Dutton and Company, 1913.

COMPILATIONS

The Wedding-Day Book. Boston, Lothrop Publishing Company, 1895.

English Drama, A Working Basis (with Lydia Bowker Godfrey). Privately printed, 1896.

English History told by English Poets (with Katharine Coman). New York, The Macmillan Company, 1902.

EDITIONS

Coleridge, Samuel Taylor. *The Rime of the Ancient Mariner.* Boston, Sibley and Company, 1889.

The Ballad Book. Chicago, Benjamin H. Sanborn and Company, 1890.

Shakespeare, William. *The Merchant of Venice.* Boston, Leach, Shewell and Sanborn, 1894.

———. *A Midsummer Night's Dream.* Boston, Leach, Shewell and Sanborn, 1895.

———. *As You Like It.* Boston, Leach, Shewell and Sanborn, 1896.

Keats, John. *The Eve of St. Agnes and Other Poems.* New York, Silver, Burdett and Company, 1902.

Mabie, Hamilton Wright. *Norse Stories Retold from the Eddas.* Chicago, Rand, McNally and Company, 1902.

Hawthorne, Nathaniel. *Romances* (Lenox Edition, 14 vols.). New York, Thomas Y. Crowell and Company, 1902.

Ruskin, John. *The King of the Golden River.* Chicago, Rand, McNally and Company, 1903.

The Poems of Alice and Phoebe Cary. New York, Thomas Y. Crowell and Company, 1903.

Tennyson, Alfred Lord. *The Princess.* New York, American Book Company, 1904.

———. *Idylls of the King* (selections). Boston, Sibley and Company, 1905.

Hawthorne, Nathaniel. *Our Old Home.* New York, Thomas Y. Crowell and Company, 1906.

Heywood, Thomas. *A Woman Killed with Kindness* and *The Fair Maid of the West* (the Belles Lettres Series). Boston, D. C. Heath and Company, 1917.

———. *The Fair Maid of the West* (the Belles Lettres Series). Boston, D. C. Heath and Company, 1917.

(The following editions were completed by Katharine Lee Bates after the death of their original editor.)

Amicis, Edmondo de. *The Heart of a Boy* (*Cuore*), *The Journal of an Italian Schoolboy* (ed. by Sophie Jewett). Chicago, Rand, McNally and Company, 1912.

Folk Ballads of Southern Europe (ed. by Sophie Jewett). New York, G. P. Putnam's Sons, 1913.

Index

Northbridge (Mass.): 5, 8, 11, 13

UNIVERSITY OF OKLAHOMA PRESS

NORMAN